THE HAL LEONARD COMPLETE
HARMONICA
METHOD

BY BOBBY JOE HOLMAN

ISBN 978-0-7935-8853-4

HAL•LEONARD®
CORPORATION
7777 W. BLUEMOUND RD. P.O. BOX 13819 MILWAUKEE, WI 53213

In Australia Contact:
Hal Leonard Australia Pty. Ltd
22 Taunton Drive P.O. Box 5130
Cheltenham East, 3192 Victoria, Australia
Email: ausadmin@halleonard.com

Visit Hal Leonard Online at
www.halleonard.com

THE HAL LEONARD COMPLETE
HARMONICA
METHOD

Introduction

◆❶ Welcome to The Hal Leonard Complete Harmonica Method—Chromatic Harmonica. To fully understand the materials in this book, I highly recommend the reader study and complete the first volume of this method: The Diatonic Harmonica (HL 00841285). It gives the student a complete overview of the fundamentals and techniques required to play all genres of music.

If you have already done this, you are now ready to take the next step and delve into the wonderful and exciting world of the chromatic harmonica!

Heart to Harp,

Bobby Joe Holman

TIP BOX

Many types of songs arranged for the chromatic harmonica can be found in the following Hal Leonard Harmonica Songbooks, available from your local music dealer:

Broadway Songs (HL00820009)
Christmas Carols and Hymns (HL00820008)
Classical Favorites (HL00820006)
Movie Favorites (HL00820014)
Pop Rock Favorites (HL00820013)
TV Favorites (HL00820007)

⊡ CHAPTER 1
How the Chromatic Harmonica Works
⊡⊡⊡⊡⊡⊡⊡⊡⊡⊡

Sound is produced in the same manner as the diatonic harmonica. Air passes over two brass reeds: one reed vibrates when air is blown (exhaled) through the harmonica and the other reed vibrates when air is drawn (inhaled) into the harmonica.

The differences between the chromatic and the diatonic harmonica are as follows:

- Construction.
- Note layout.
- Tonality.
- Holding the chromatic.

Construction

The chromatic is actually two harmonicas in one, due to the slide that completely changes the notes. When the slide is out (the rest position), the chromatic harmonica is tuned to the key of C. When the slide is pushed in, the chromatic is tuned one-half step above to C♯. This gives the chromatic the potential to be played in *any* major or minor key. The difference between the various chromatic harmonicas is the number of octaves they cover.

Note Range

There are basically five Hohner chromatic harmonicas:

- Chrometta #250—two octaves.
- Chromonica #260—two and one-half octaves.
- Super Chromonica #270—three octaves.
- Chrometta #255—three octaves.
- Super "64" Chromonica #280—four octaves.

Tonality

Due to its construction, the air chamber, reeds and mouthpiece on the chromatic is potentially two to four times the size of the diatonic. This creates a distinct tone that is much bigger and warmer than the diatonic.

Holding the Chromatic

Fig. 1A shows the left-hand position for holding the chromatic harmonica. Fig. 1B shows the starting hand position for holding the chromatic. To push in the slide, position the index finger on your right hand so that the fleshy area between your first and second knuckle is over the tip of the slide.

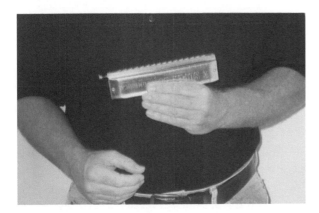

Fig. 1A

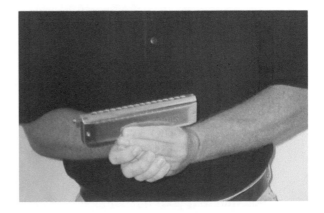

Fig. 1B

Notation Chart for Hohner Chromatic Harmonicas

◧◧◧◧◧◧◧◧◧◧

Hohner Chromatic Harmonicas have a range from two to four complete chromatic octaves. The following chart shows the notes on the staff and their position by hole number for each chromatic model. This chart is a valuable aid, particularly for the beginner until he or she becomes fully acquainted with the instrument.

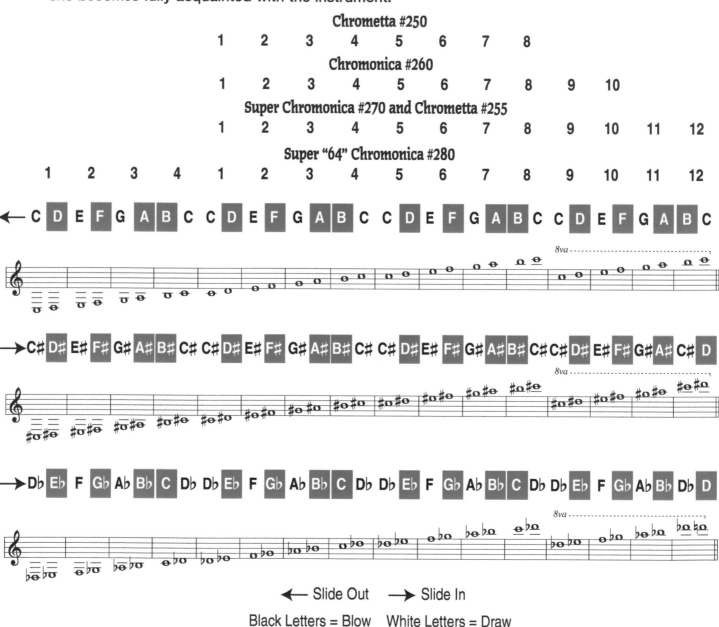

← Slide Out   → Slide In

Black Letters = Blow   White Letters = Draw

◧

TIP BOX

The chromatic is a large and cumbersome instrument compared to the diatonic, therefore requiring more patience and dexterity to play.

Practice pushing the slide in until you find the most comfortable and efficient position for your right hand.

If you find that your index finger is not long enough to reach the slide lever as described on page 5, use the area just below the tip of your index finger.

◧◧◧◧◧◧◧◧◧◧

Producing a Sound

L L L L L L L L L L

A thorough explanation of two methods for playing a single note on the diatonic harmonica can be found in the Hal Leonard Complete Harmonica Method—Diatonic Harmonica:

- pucker (p. 12).
- tongue blocking (p. 26).

These two methods, along with the *curled tongue* method, can be applied to the chromatic with the same successful results.

The Curled Tongue Method

To produce a single note using the curled tongue method, you curl your tongue as in Fig. 2A.

Fig. 2A

After practicing this technique, simply place your curled tongue on the mouthpiece of the chromatic, making sure that your tongue is only over one hole, as in Fig. 2B.

Fig. 2B

Playing the Blues on the Chromatic Harmonica

If you are unfamiliar with the concept of cross harp (second position, or Mixolydian mode) and playing in the Dorian mode (third position), please refer to the Hal Leonard Complete Harmonica Method—Diatonic Harmonica. The same basic techniques apply to the chromatic.

- To play the Mixolydian mode (or cross harp) for major key blues, play in the second position. On a C harmonica, this puts your music in the key of G.

- To play the Dorian mode for a minor blues, play in the third position. On a C harmonica, this puts your music in the key of Dm.

- When you push the slide in, you automatically move to the key of C♯, making it posible to play the second position of C♯ (G♯) and the third position of C♯ (D♯m).

Harmonica Legend

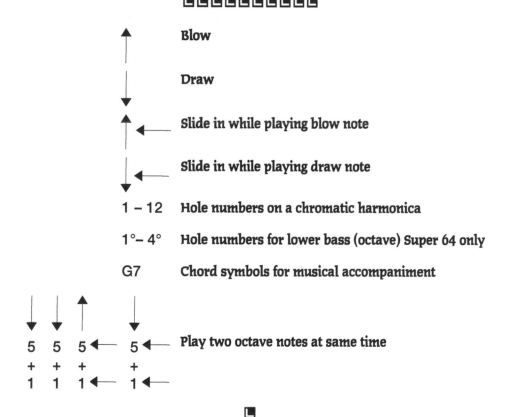

↑ Blow	
↓ Draw	
↑← Slide in while playing blow note	
↓← Slide in while playing draw note	
1 – 12	Hole numbers on a chromatic harmonica
1°– 4°	Hole numbers for lower bass (octave) Super 64 only
G7	Chord symbols for musical accompaniment

Play two octave notes at same time

TIP BOX

Do not attempt to bend notes on the chromatic harmonica. While it can be done, you risk damaging an expensive instrument.

Use the slide to bend "up" one half step.

The Hohner Harmonica Company makes chromatic harmonicas in all keys if you wish to play blues in second and third positions, as you would on a diatonic harmonica. The advantage is that you would be able to enjoy the warmer and more colorful tones of the chromatic.

Dixie

By Dan Emmett

Key: C major
All Chromatic Harmonicas
Curled Tongue

Brightly

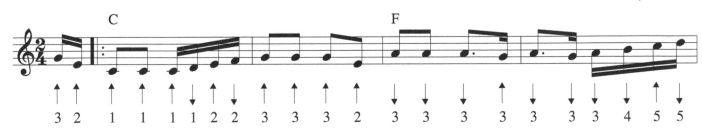

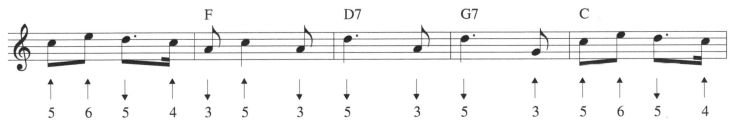

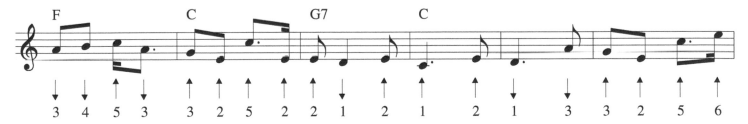

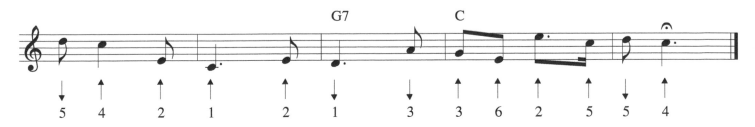

TIP BOX

To play a single note in the higher registers, use the pucker method.

To play octaves, use the tongue blocking method.

To play a single note in the lower register, use the curled tongue method.

You can use the curled tongue method to play the diatonic, but you must not touch your tongue to the harmonica. Instead, hold it slightly away while you blow.

Brahms Lullaby

By Johannes Brahms

Key: E♭ major
All Chromatic Harmonicas

Slowly

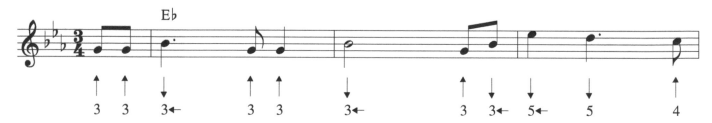

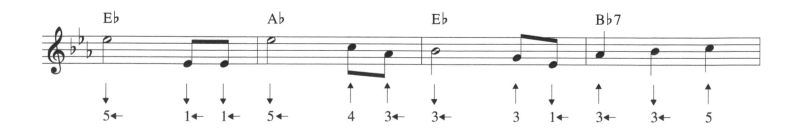

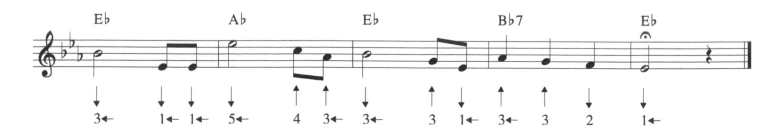

House of the Rising Sun

Traditional

Key: A minor
Fourth Position
Harmonica: Chromatic Super 64 only

Additional Lyrics

2. If I had listened to what mama said,
I'd 'a' been at home today.
Being so young and foolish, poor girl,
Let a gambler lead me astray.

3. My mother, she's a tailor,
She sells those new blue jeans.
My Sweetheart, he's a drunkard, Lord,
Drinks down in New Orleans.

4. The only thing a drunkard needs
Is a suitcase and a trunk.
The only time he's satisfied
Is when he's on a drunk.

5. Go tell my baby, sister,
Never do like I have done.
To shun that house in New Orleans,
They call the Rising Sun.

6. One foot is on the platform,
And the other one on the train.
I'm going back to New Orleans
To wear that ball and chain.

7. I'm going back to New Orleans,
My race is almost run.
Going back to end my life
Beneath the Rising Sun.

Malibu
Music by Bobby Joe Holman

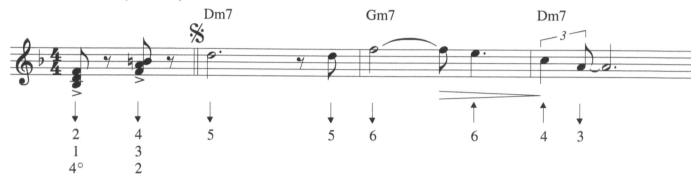

Key: D minor (Dorian)
Third Position
Harmonica: Chromatic Super 64 only

Slow Blues (12/8 feel)

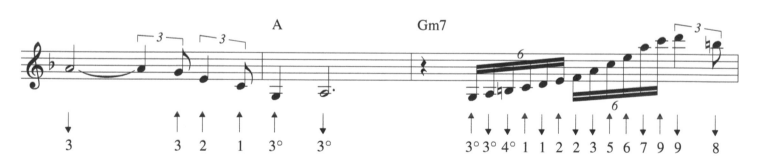

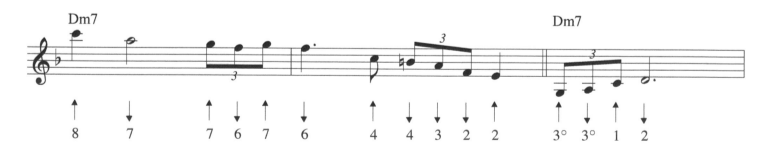

D.S. ad lib.

Octaves

Playing octaves on the chromatic harmonica can be an extremely rewarding experience. As noted, the chromatic has a richer, warmer tone than the diatonic harmonica. When you add the fullness that only octaves can impart, you truly have a magnificent sound at your fingertips.

Due to the note layout of the chromatic, it is relatively easy to play octaves. If you will look at the Notation Chart on page 6, you will see that *all* the blow and draw notes repeat every five holes. Therefore, you will need to cover five holes with your mouth. Place your tongue over holes 2, 3 and 4, leaving holes 1 and 5 clear for the air to pass through. Remember that you can do this anywhere on any chromatic harmonica and you will be playing octaves.

TIP BOX

Knowing the name of the lower note (to the left) will give you the name of the octave.
Your tongue and lips must make a good, tight seal for the clearest tone.

Amazing Grace

Traditional

Key: C major
Harmonica: All chromatic harmonicas

Slowly

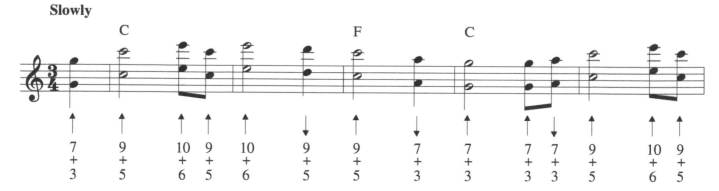

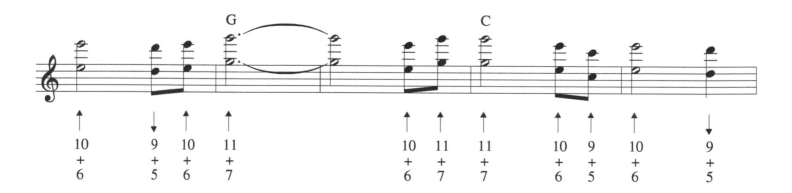

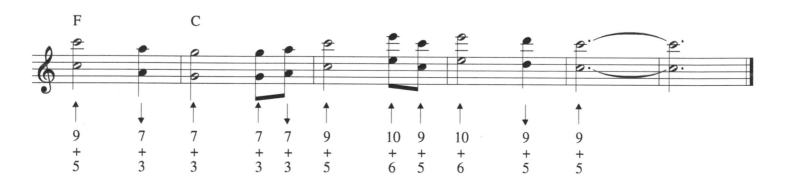

CHAPTER 2
Learning to Play
Major and Minor Diatonic Scales
◨◨◨◨◨◨◨◨◨◨

The next section deals with the complete mastery of the most important scales for the chromatic harmonica. Learning and playing these scales is not as difficult as you might imagine. The following system will simplify the process for you.

- A song will be presented to go along with each scale in the key of C.

- An easy to understand explanation of how to apply the scale will accompany each one.

- The play-along CD includes two tracks per song: a version with harp and accompaniment and a practice track with accompaniment only.

- Each scale in every key will be found in the Appendix (p. 43).

◨

TIP BOX
Refer to the notation chart on page 6 when learning each new scale.
As you study each scale, mentally play through it in your head.
To be able to play through two full octaves for each scale in all keys, you should have the Super Chromonica #270, Chrometta #255 or the "64" Chronomica #280.

◨◨◨◨◨◨◨◨◨◨

◨

C Ionian Mode Song
◨◨◨◨◨◨◨◨◨◨

TIP BOX

The Ionian Mode (a.k.a. major scale) is played in major key songs or specifically over major triads, major 6, major 7 or major 9 chords.

It is also known as the diatonic scale or the "do, re, mi" scale.

All other scales are derived from the major scale.

The major scale is the most common scale found in popular music.

G Ionian Mode Song

D Ionian Mode Song

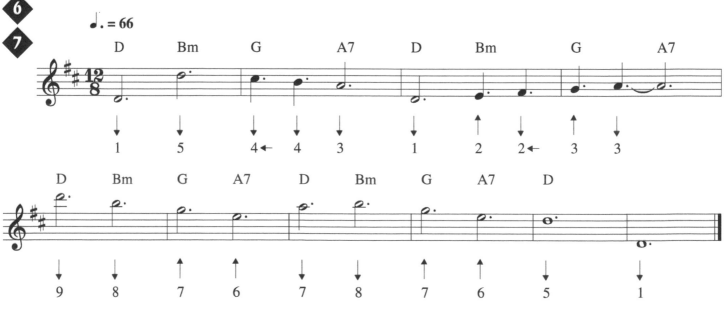

C Dorian Mode Song

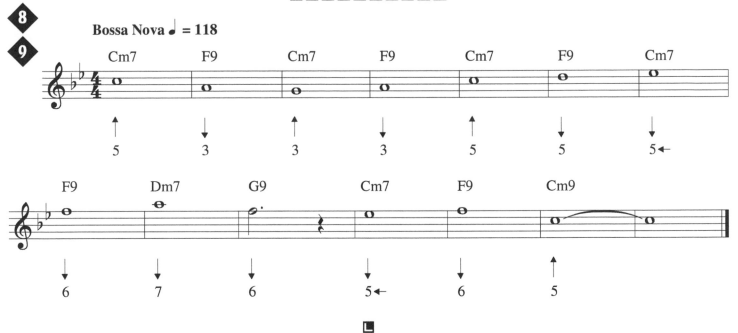

TIP BOX

The Dorian mode is played in minor key songs with minor 7 chords, and in songs where the I chord is minor and the IV chord is major.
It is commonly used in jazz, blues, rock and pop songs.

G Dorian Mode Song

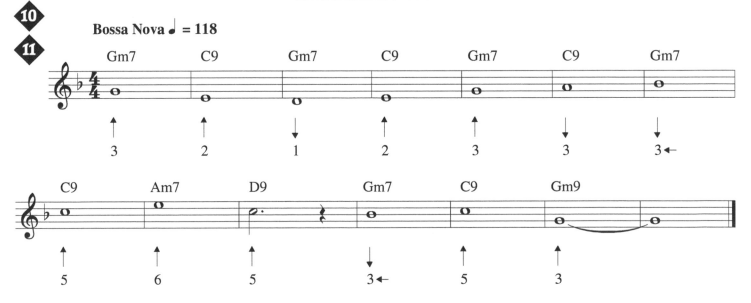

D Dorian Mode Song

C Phrygian Mode Song

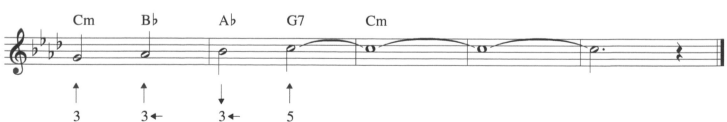

TIP BOX

The Phrygian mode is played in minor key songs where an "exotic" flavor is desired.
It is used extensively in jazz.

G Phrygian Mode Song

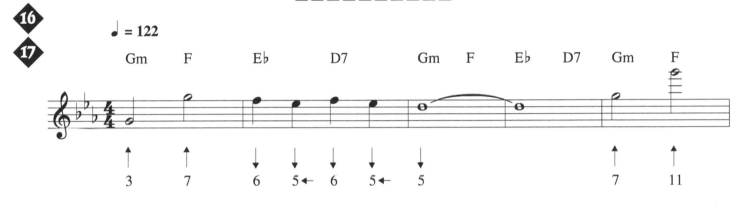

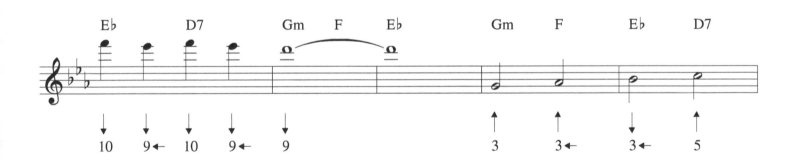

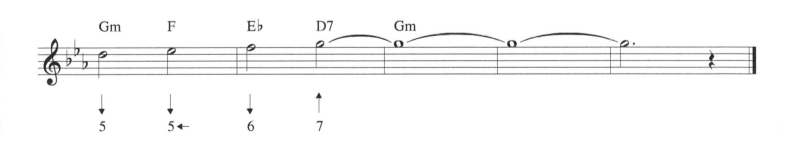

D Phrygian Mode Song

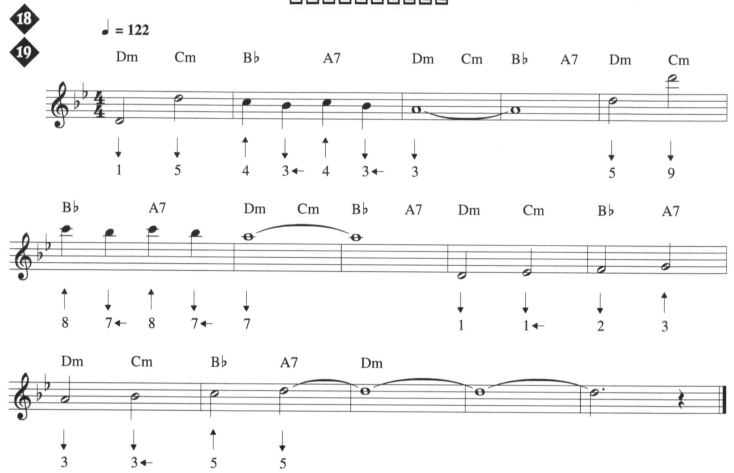

C Lydian Mode Song

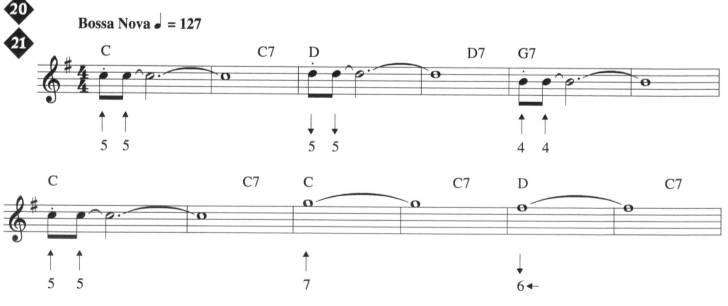

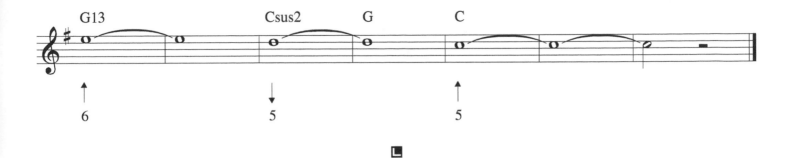

TIP BOX

The Lydian mode is played in major key songs when a "jazzy" flavor is desired.

G Lydian Mode Song

Bossa Nova ♩ = 127

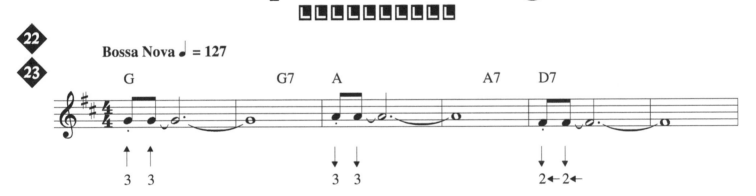

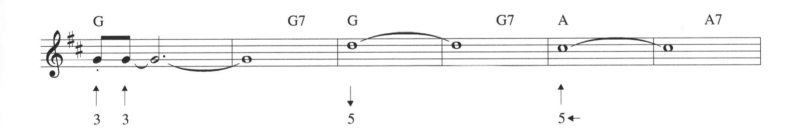

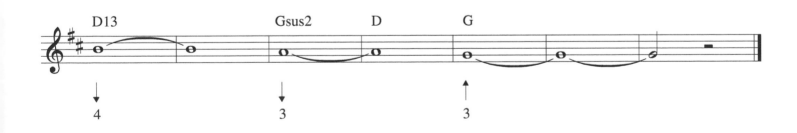

D Lydian Mode Song

C Mixolydian Mode Song

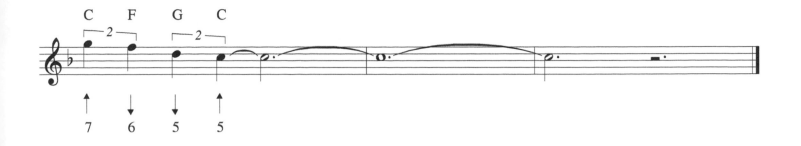

G Mixolydian Mode Song

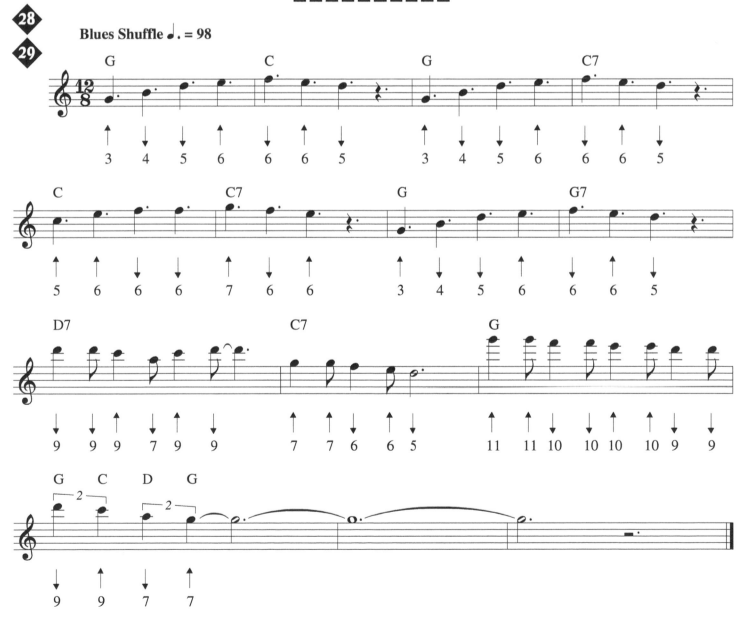

D Mixolydian Mode Song

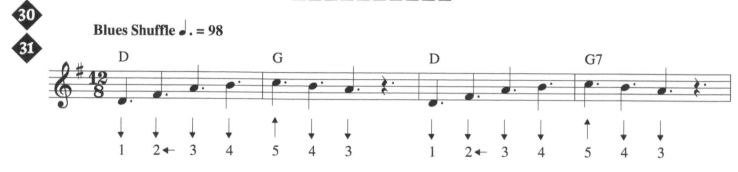

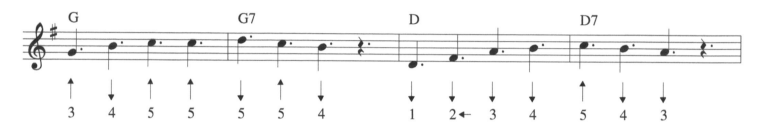

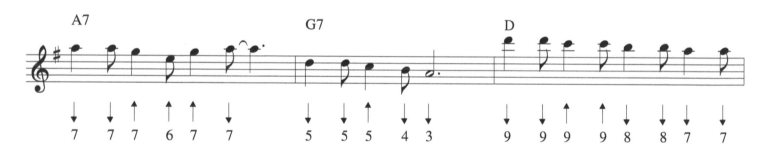

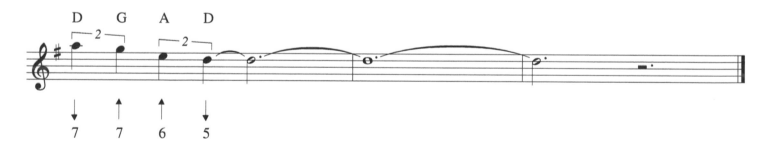

C Aeolian Mode Song

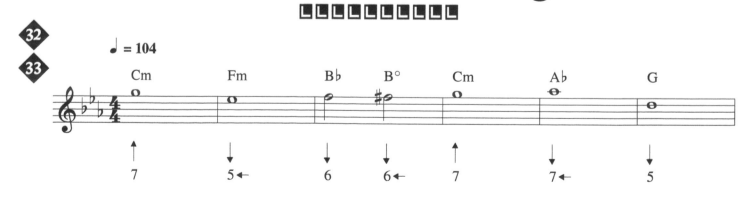

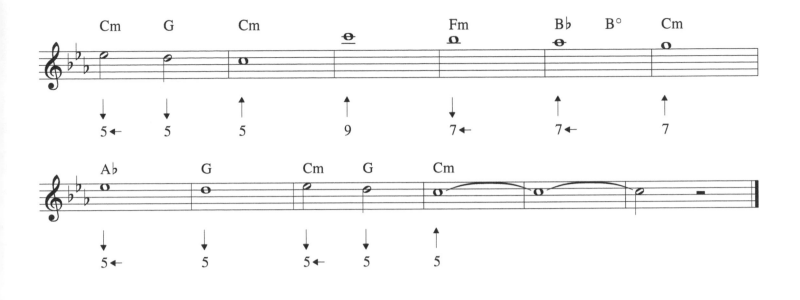

TIP BOX

The Aeolian mode is used in minor key songs, specifically over minor triads and in minor key songs where the I and IV chords are minor.

It is also known as the "natural minor" scale or the "relative minor" scale.

It is used extensively in all forms of music.

G Aeolian Mode Song

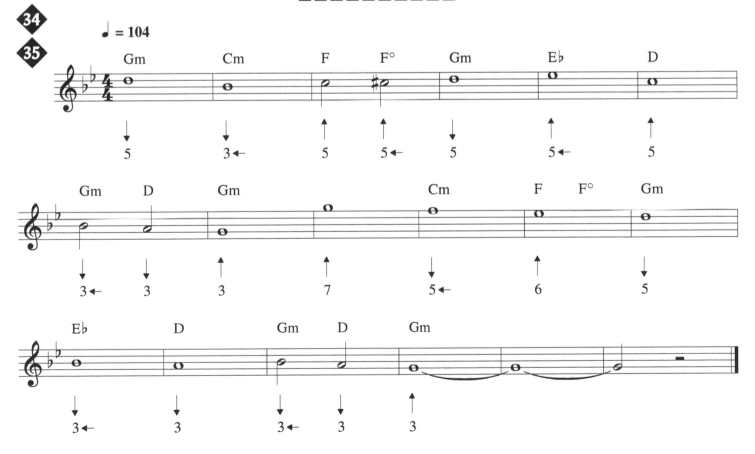

D Aeolian Mode Song

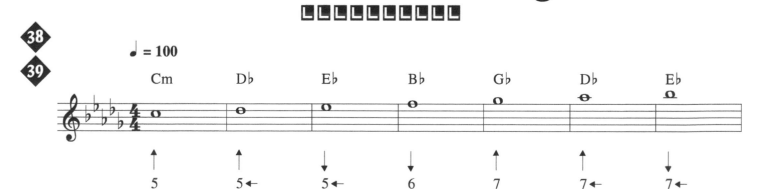

C Locrian Mode Song

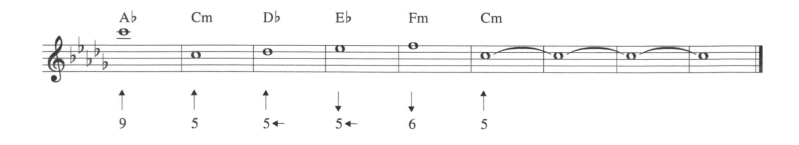

TIP BOX

The Locrian mode can also be played over diminished chords
when a "dark" flavor is desired.

It is used mainly in jazz.

G Locrian Mode Song

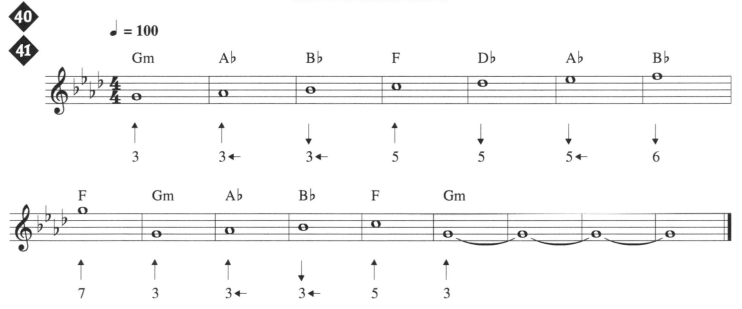

D Locrian Mode Song

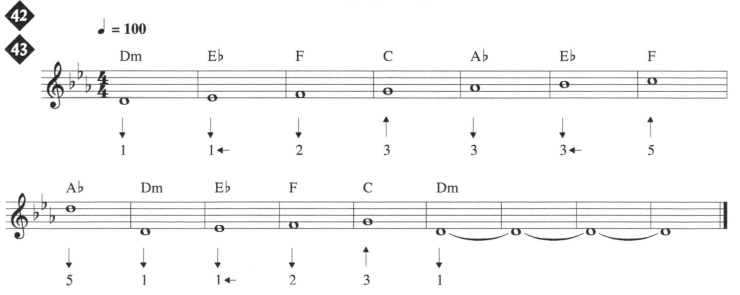

C Harmonic Minor Scale Song

G Harmonic Minor Scale Song

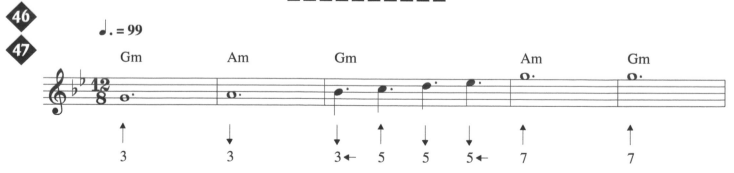

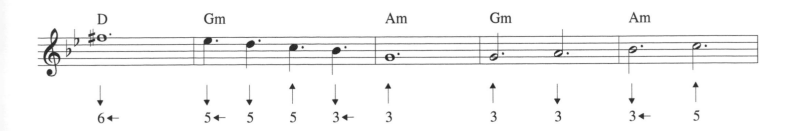

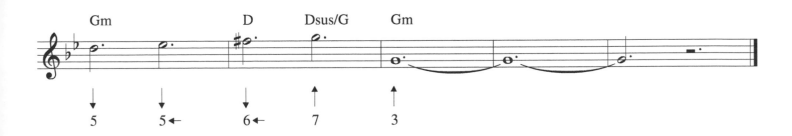

D Harmonic Minor Scale Song

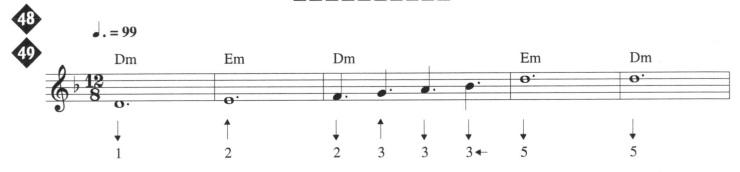

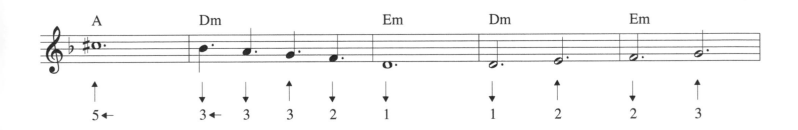

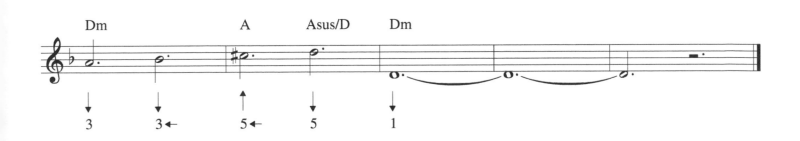

L

C Jazz Melodic Minor Scale Song

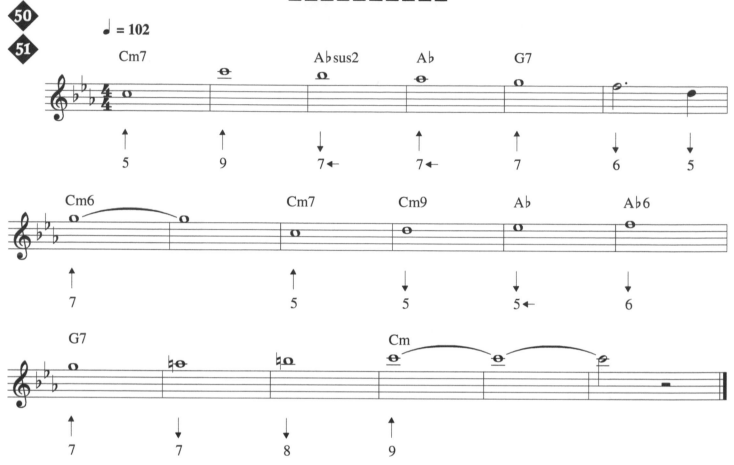

L

TIP BOX

The Jazz Melodic Minor scale is played in minor key songs, specifically with minor triads or minor 6 chords when a "jazzy" flavor is desired.

G Jazz Melodic Minor Scale Song

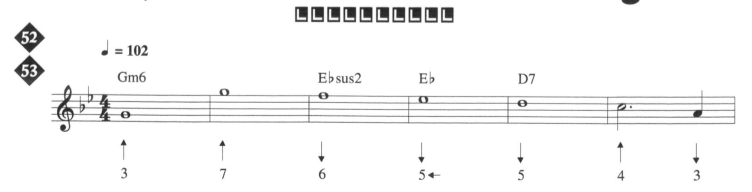

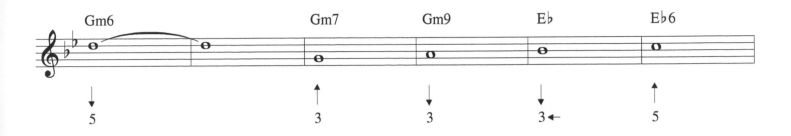

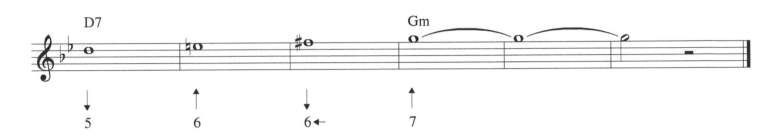

D Jazz Melodic Minor Scale Song

54
55

♩ = 102

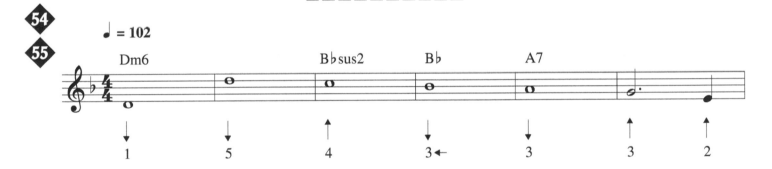

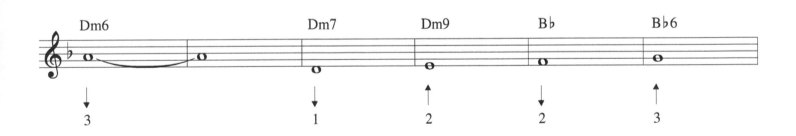

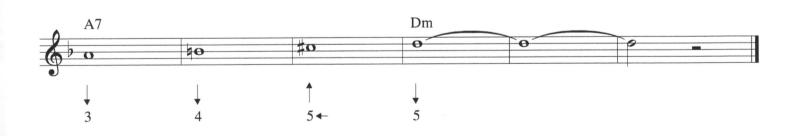

C Major Pentatonic Scale Song

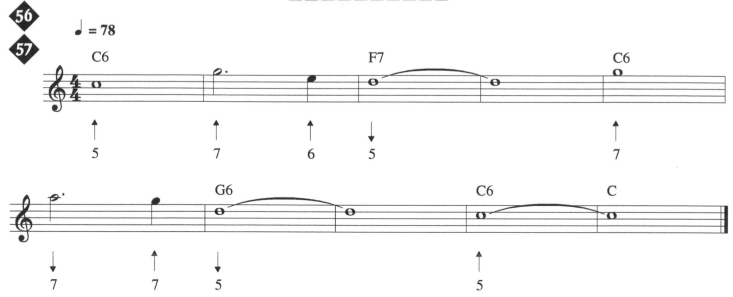

TIP BOX

The Major Pentatonic scale is played in major key songs when simple melodies are desired.
It is used most often in rock, pop and blues.

G Major Pentatonic Scale Song

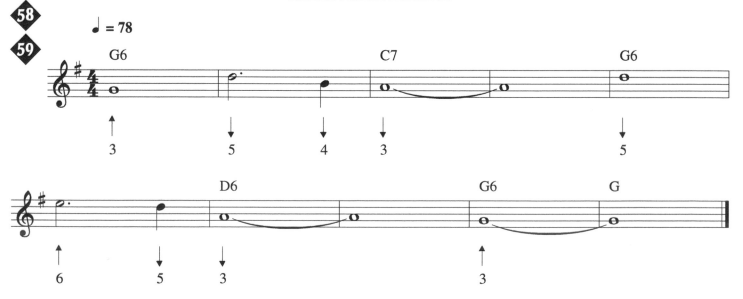

D Major Pentatonic Scale Song

C Minor Pentatonic Blues Scale Song

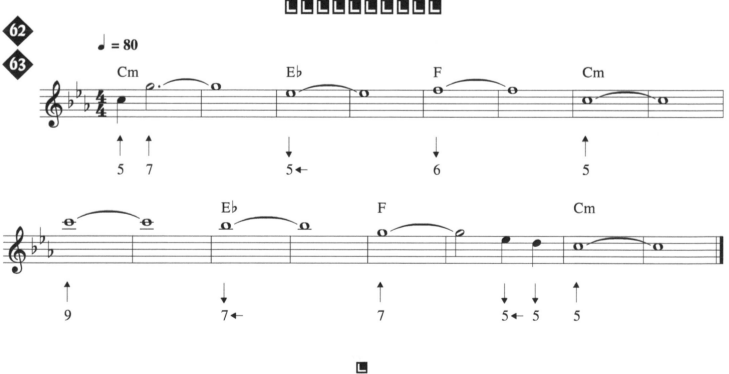

TIP BOX

The Minor Pentatonic Blues scale can be played in major or minor key songs with simple I, IV and V chord changes.

It is used extensively in blues and rock.

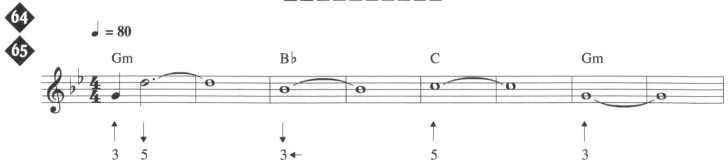

G Minor Pentatonic Blues Scale Song

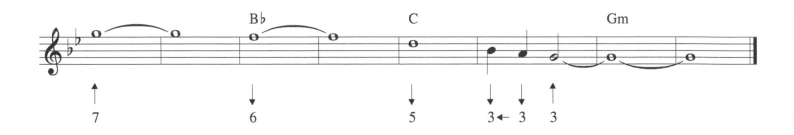

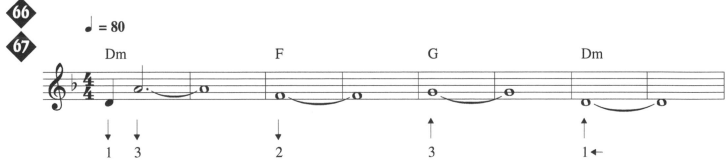

D Minor Pentatonic Blues Scale Song

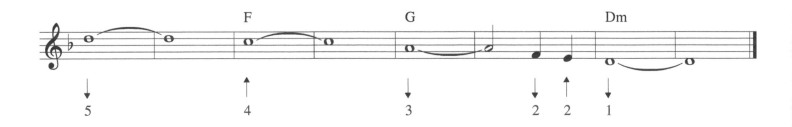

C Blues Scale Song
□□□□□□□□□

TIP BOX

The Blues scale is played in major and minor key songs based around the
I, IV and V chord changes.
It is used extensively in blues and blues/rock music.

□□□□□□□□□□

□
G Blues Scale Song
□□□□□□□□□

L
D Blues Scale Song
L L L L L L L L L L

L
C Whole Tone Scale Song
L L L L L L L L L L

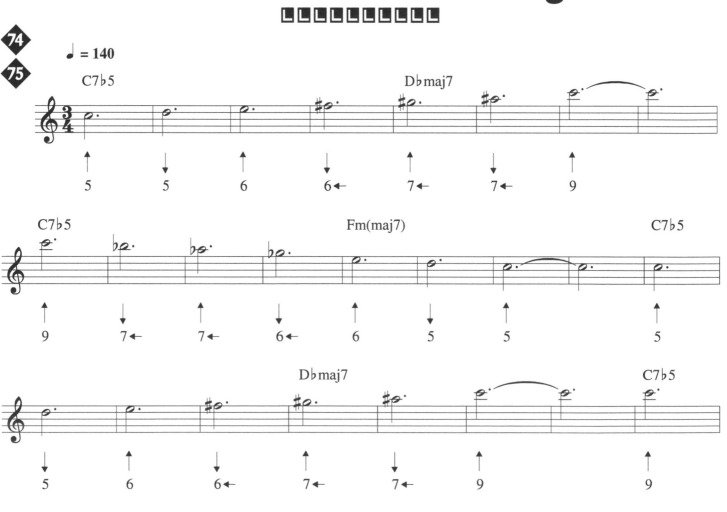

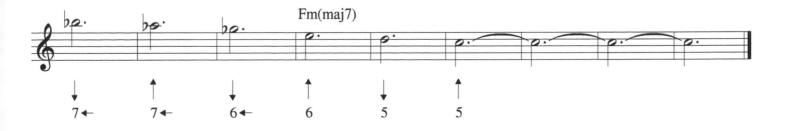

TIP BOX
The Whole Tone scale is played over augmented triads, 7♭5 and 7♯5 chords.
It is used mostly in jazz or progressive rock.

G Whole Tone Scale Song

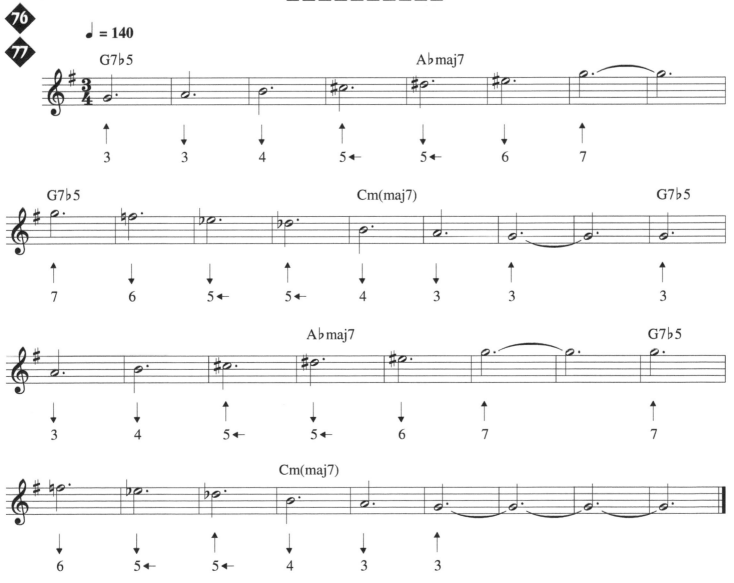

D Whole Tone Scale Song

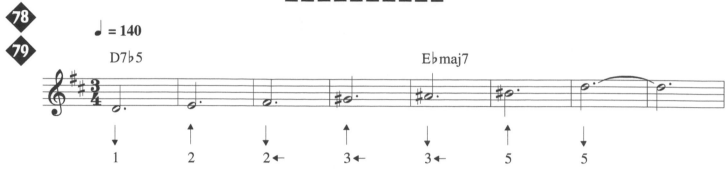

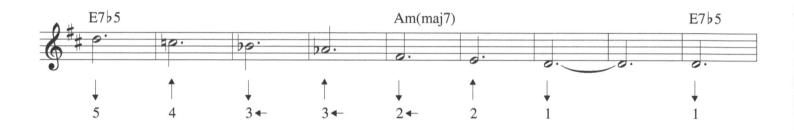

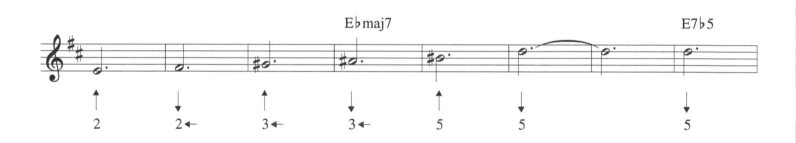

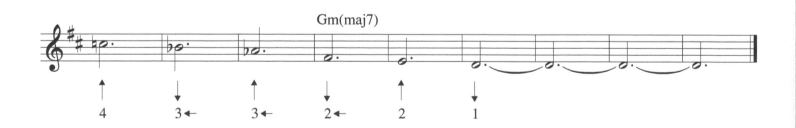

C Chromatic Scale Song

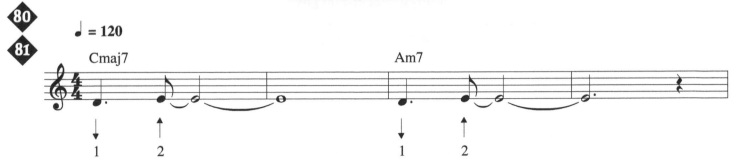

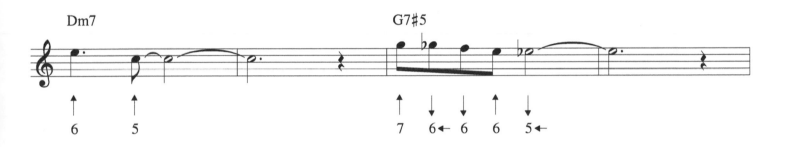

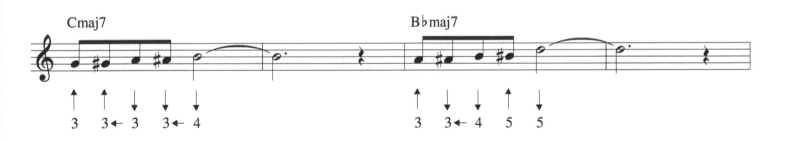

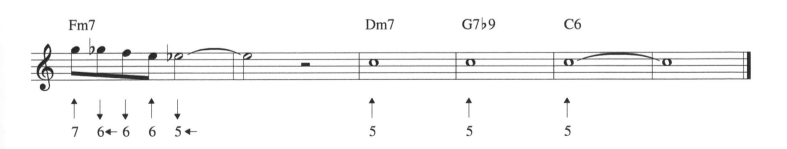

TIP BOX

The Chromatic scale is used for "ornamentation" or "extra" notes to fill out the major scale.
It is used mostly in jazz and progressive rock.

G Chromatic Scale Song

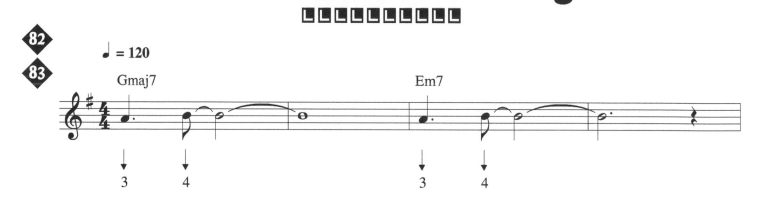

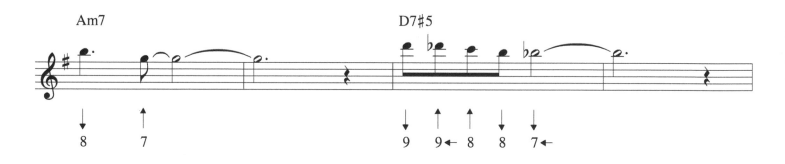

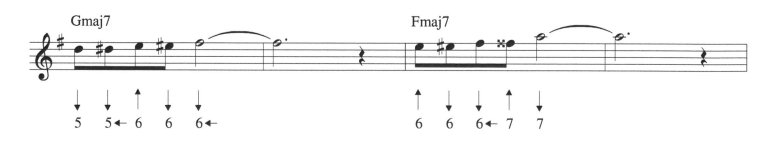

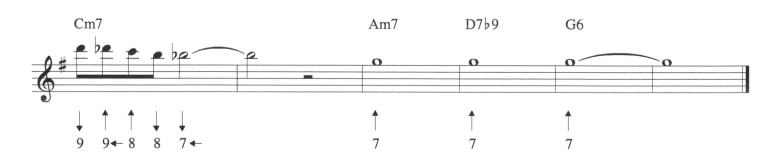

D Chromatic Scale Song

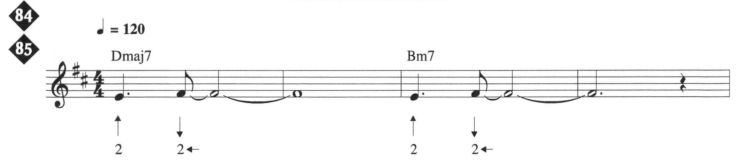

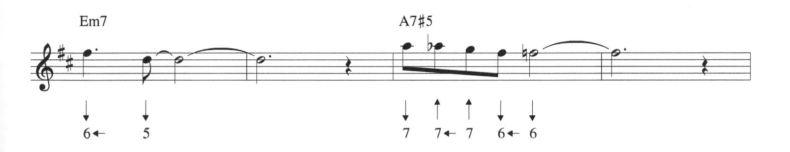

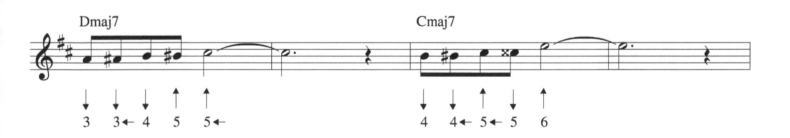

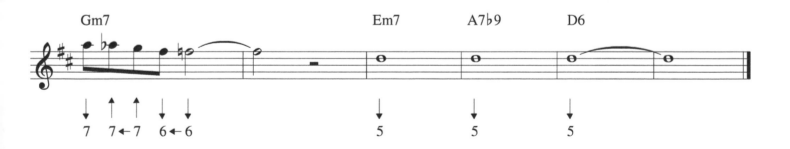

Octave Scale Song

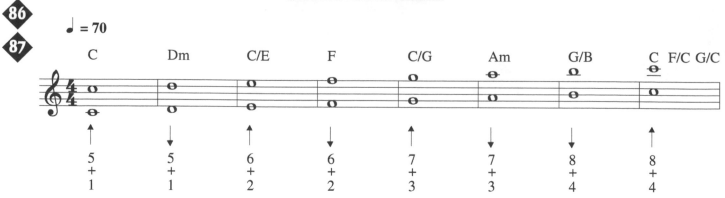

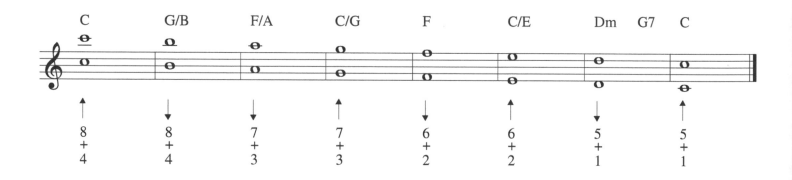

Appendix

C Major Scale

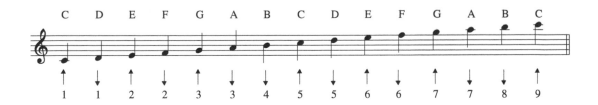

C Dorian Mode

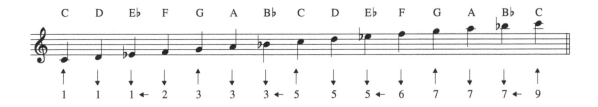

C Phrygian Mode

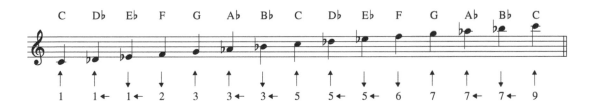

C Lydian Mode

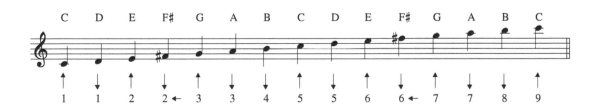

C Mixolydian Mode

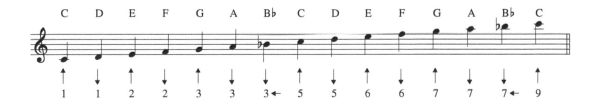

C Aeolian Mode

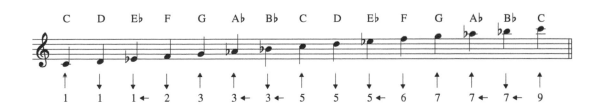

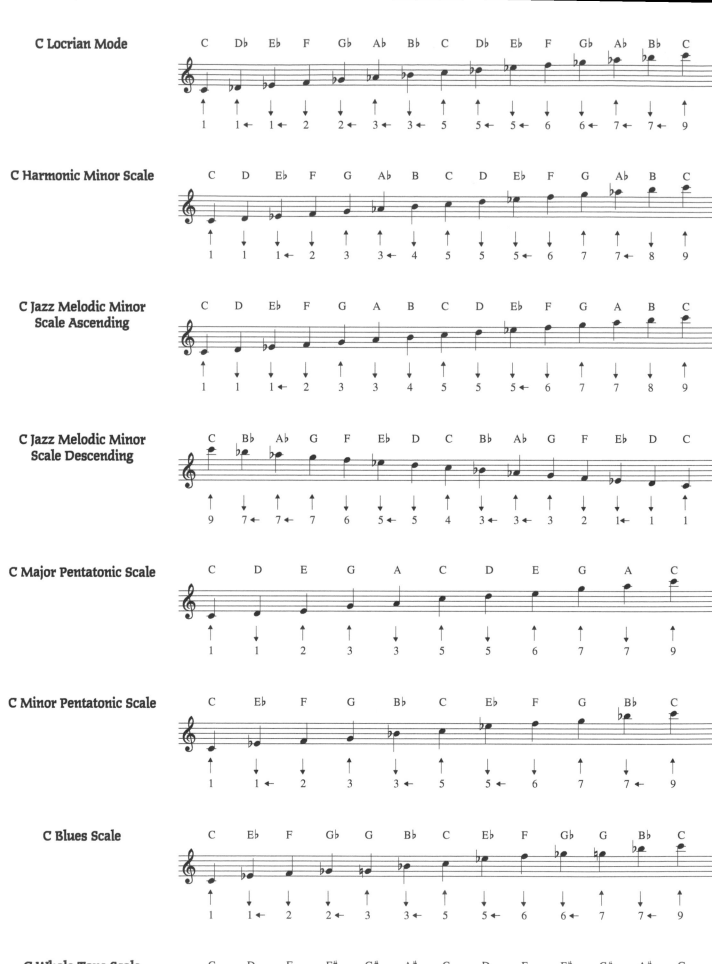

C Chromatic Scale

L L L L L L L L L

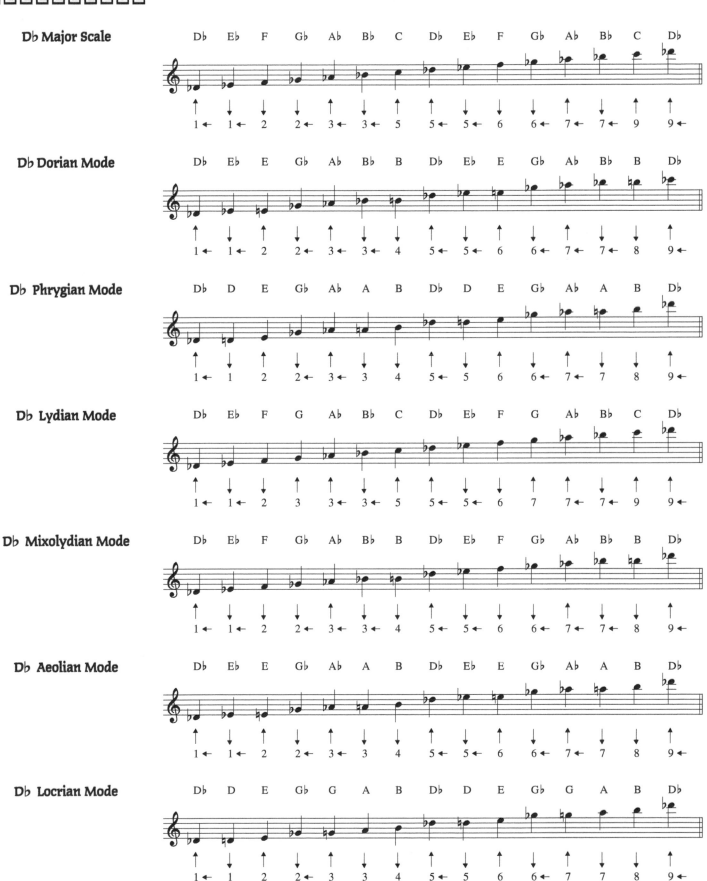

Db Major Scale

Db Dorian Mode

Db Phrygian Mode

Db Lydian Mode

Db Mixolydian Mode

Db Aeolian Mode

Db Locrian Mode

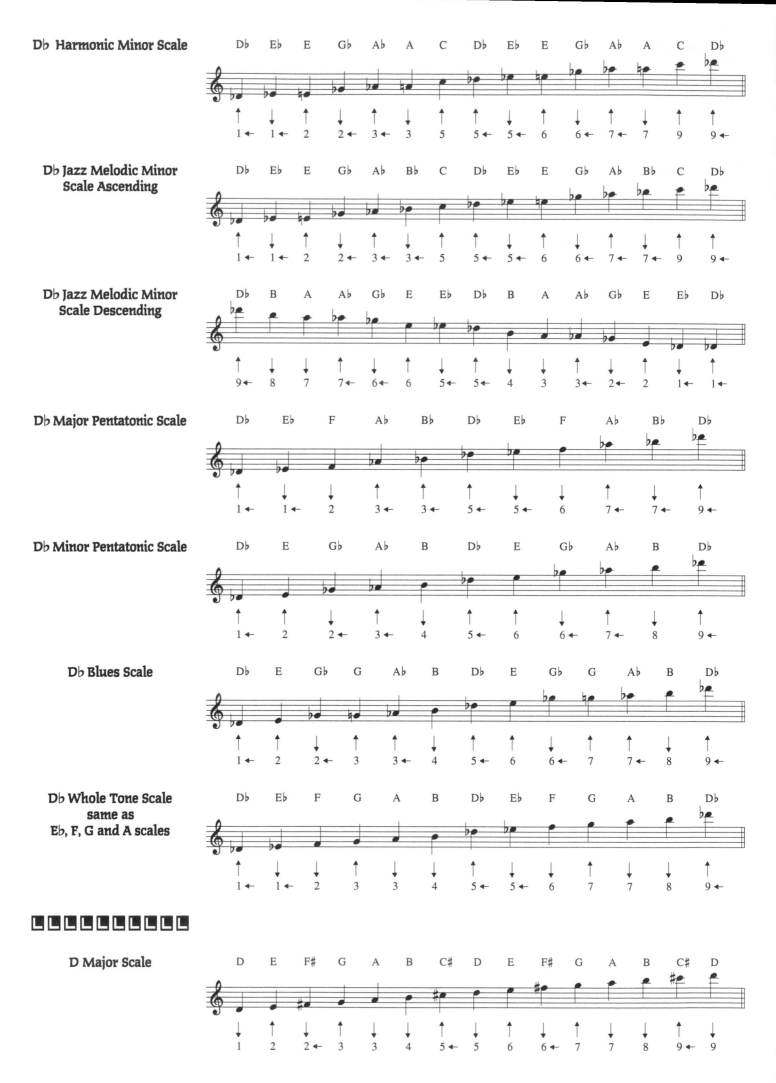

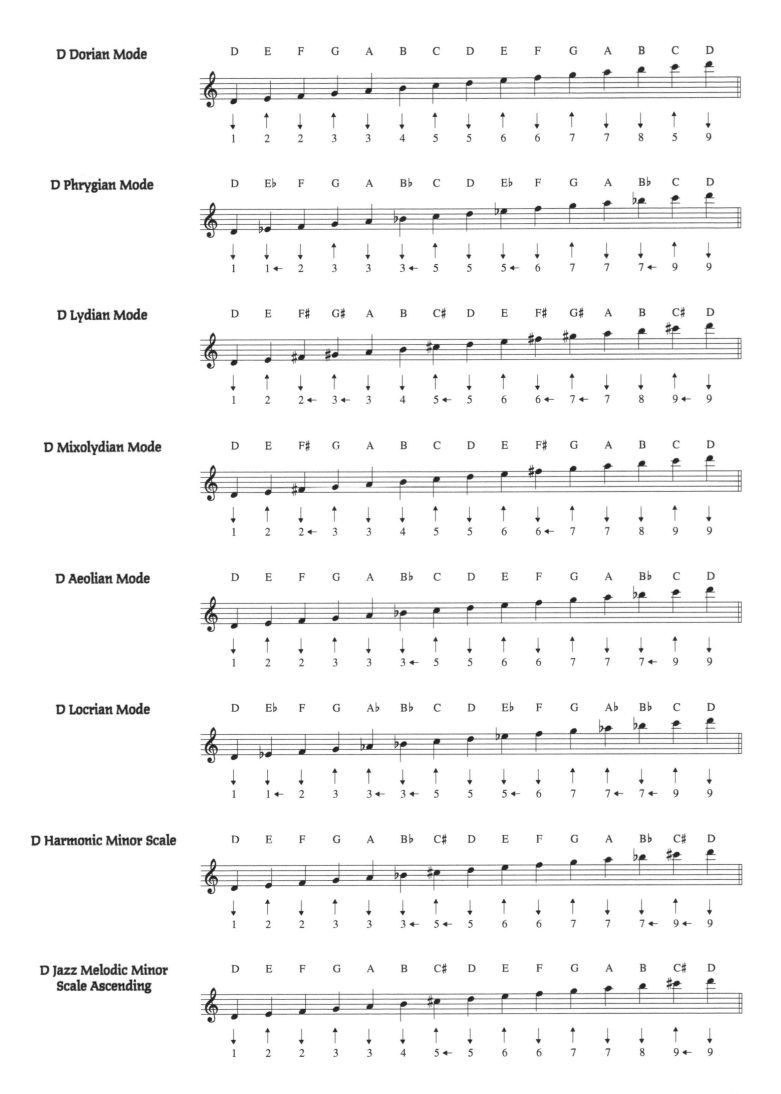

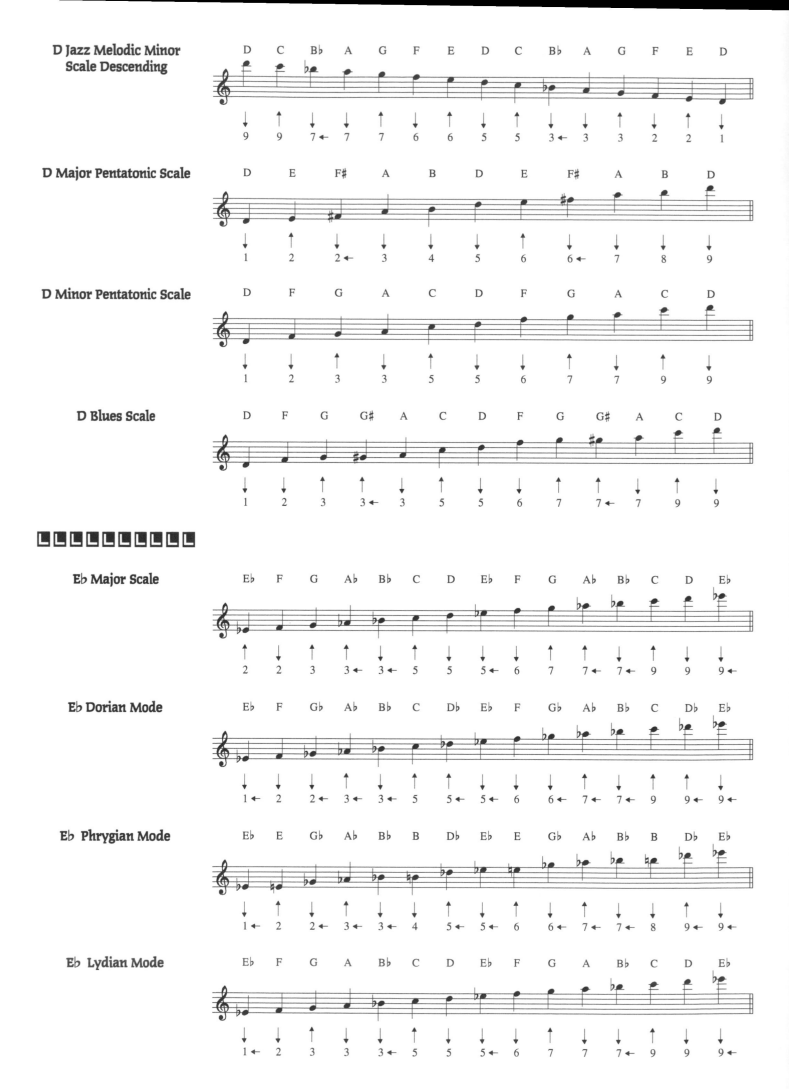

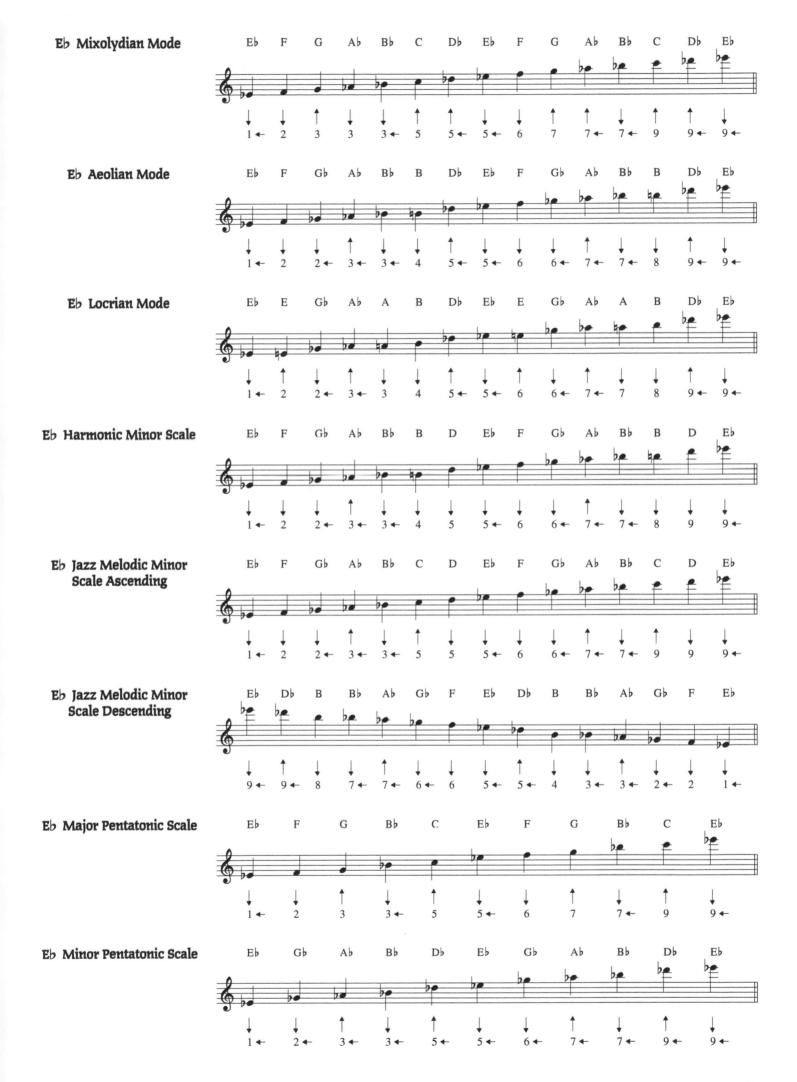

Eb Blues Scale

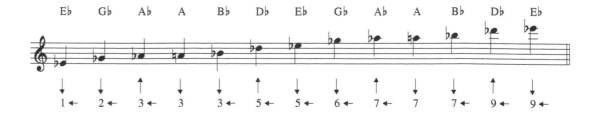

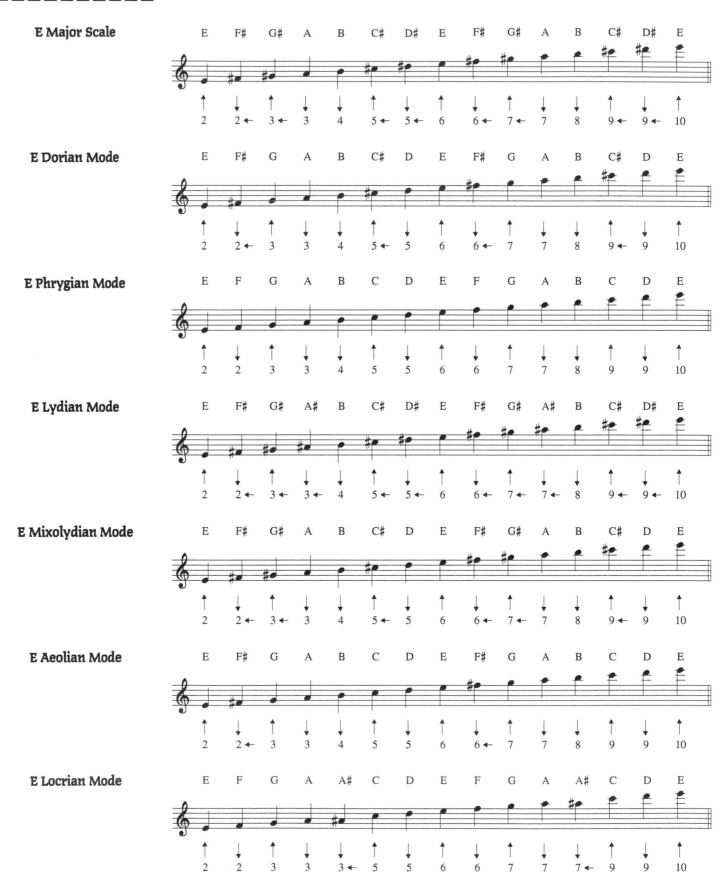

E Harmonic Minor Scale

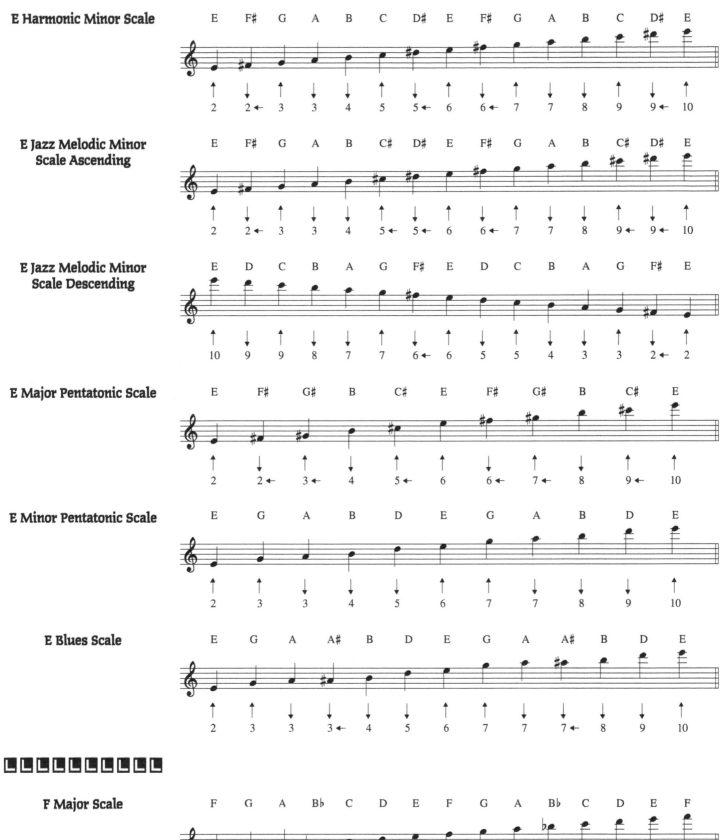

E Jazz Melodic Minor Scale Ascending

E Jazz Melodic Minor Scale Descending

E Major Pentatonic Scale

E Minor Pentatonic Scale

E Blues Scale

F Major Scale

F Dorian Mode

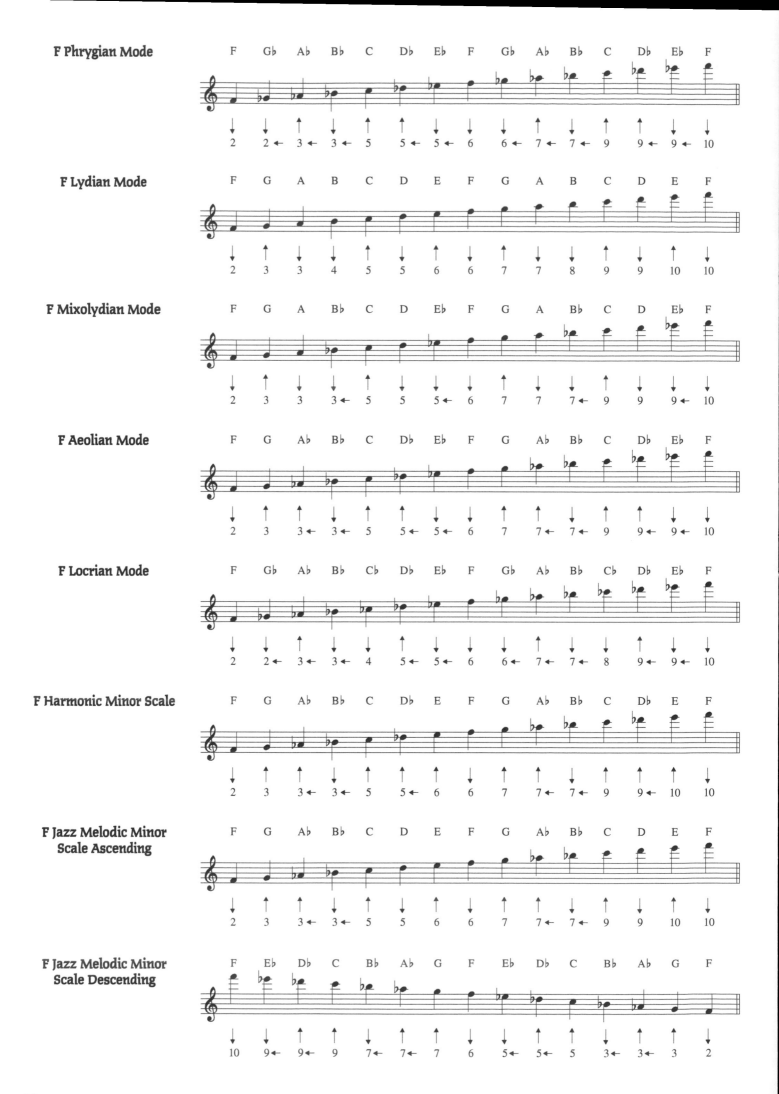

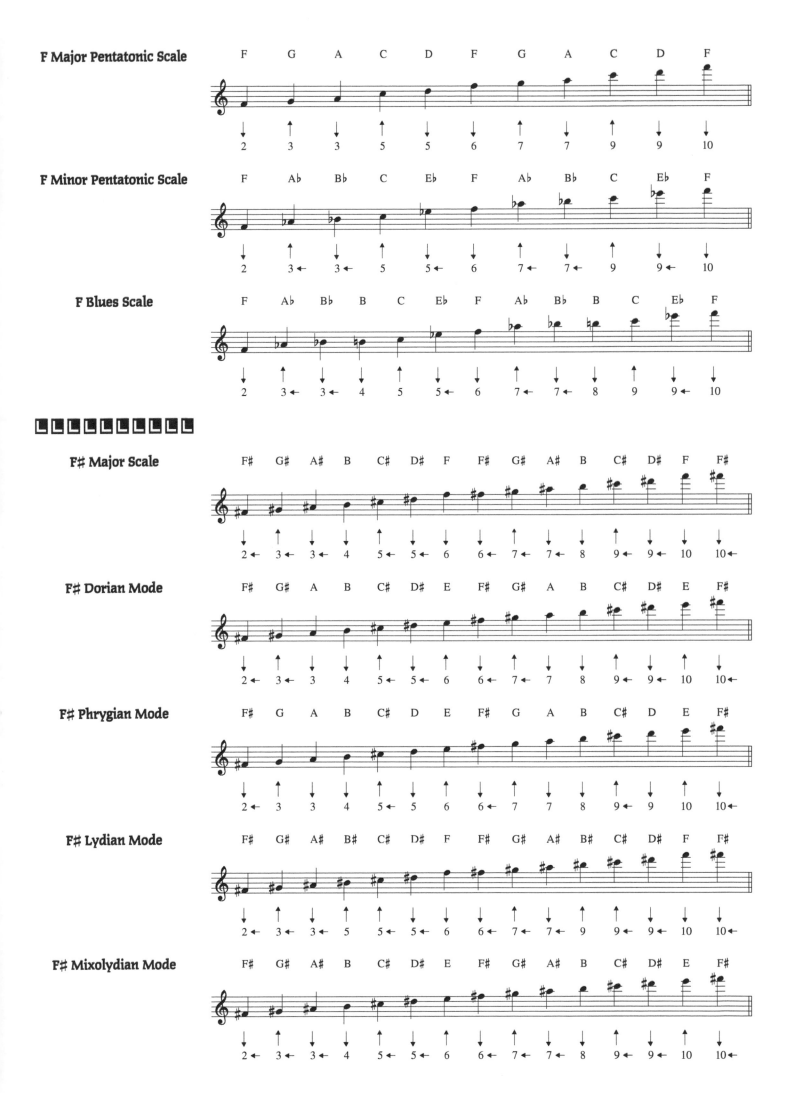

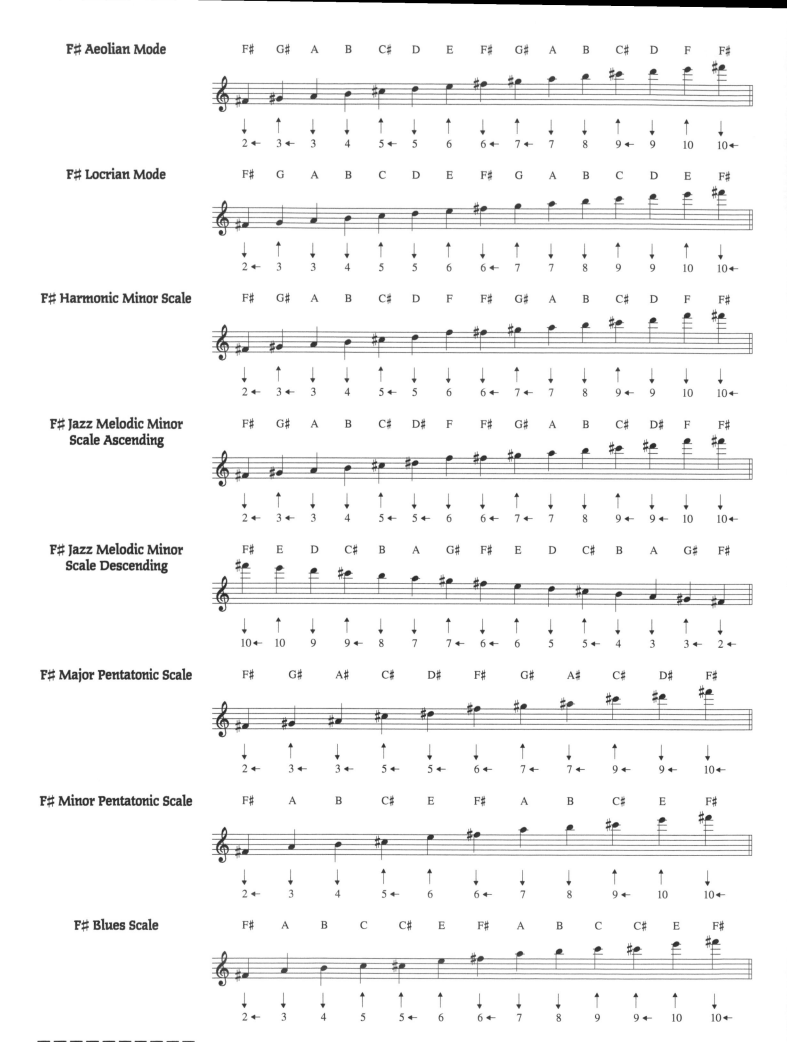

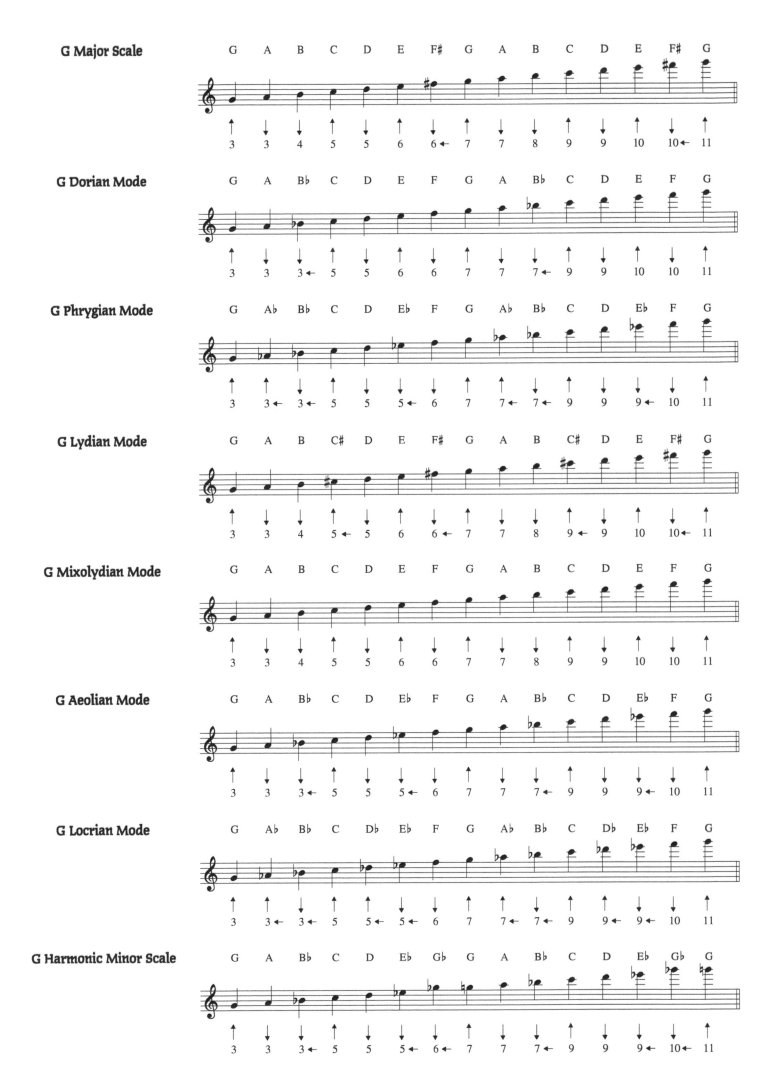

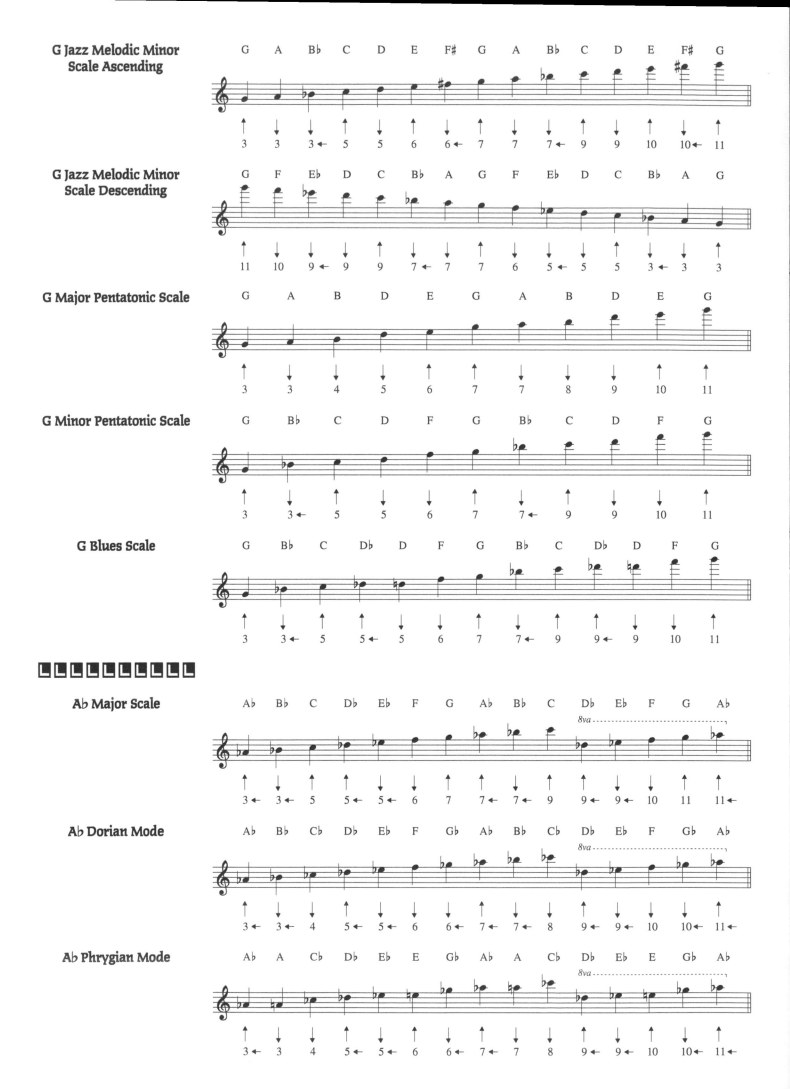

G Jazz Melodic Minor Scale Ascending
G A Bb C D E F# G A Bb C D E F# G
↑ ↓ ↓ ↑ ↓ ↑ ↑ ↓ ↓ ↑ ↓ ↑ ↓ ↑
3 3 3← 5 5 6 6← 7 7 7← 9 9 10 10← 11

G Jazz Melodic Minor Scale Descending
G F Eb D C Bb A G F Eb D C Bb A G
↑ ↓ ↓ ↓ ↓ ↑ ↓ ↑ ↓ ↓ ↓ ↓ ↓ ↓ ↑
11 10 9← 9 9 7← 7 7 6 5← 5 5 3← 3 3

G Major Pentatonic Scale
G A B D E G A B D E G
↑ ↓ ↓ ↓ ↑ ↑ ↓ ↓ ↓ ↑ ↑
3 3 4 5 6 7 7 8 9 10 11

G Minor Pentatonic Scale
G Bb C D F G Bb C D F G
↑ ↓ ↑ ↓ ↓ ↑ ↓ ↑ ↓ ↓ ↑
3 3← 5 5 6 7 7← 9 9 10 11

G Blues Scale
G Bb C Db D F G Bb C Db D F G
↑ ↓ ↑ ↓ ↓ ↑ ↓ ↑ ↓ ↑ ↓ ↓ ↑
3 3← 5 5← 5 6 7 7← 9 9← 9 10 11

LLLLLLLLLL

Ab Major Scale
Ab Bb C Db Eb F G Ab Bb C Db Eb F G Ab
↑ ↓ ↑ ↑ ↓ ↓ ↑ ↑ ↓ ↓ ↑ ↓ ↓ ↑ ↑
3← 3← 5 5← 5← 6 7 7← 7← 9 9← 9← 10 11 11←

8va --------

Ab Dorian Mode
Ab Bb Cb Db Eb F Gb Ab Bb Cb Db Eb F Gb Ab
↑ ↓ ↓ ↑ ↓ ↓ ↑ ↑ ↓ ↓ ↑ ↓ ↓ ↓ ↑
3← 3← 4 5← 5← 6 6← 7← 7← 8 9← 9← 10 10← 11←

8va --------

Ab Phrygian Mode
Ab A Cb Db Eb E Gb Ab A Cb Db Eb E Gb Ab
↑ ↓ ↓ ↑ ↓ ↓ ↑ ↑ ↓ ↓ ↑ ↓ ↓ ↓ ↑
3← 3 4 5← 5← 6 6← 7← 7 8 9← 9← 10 10← 11←

8va --------

56

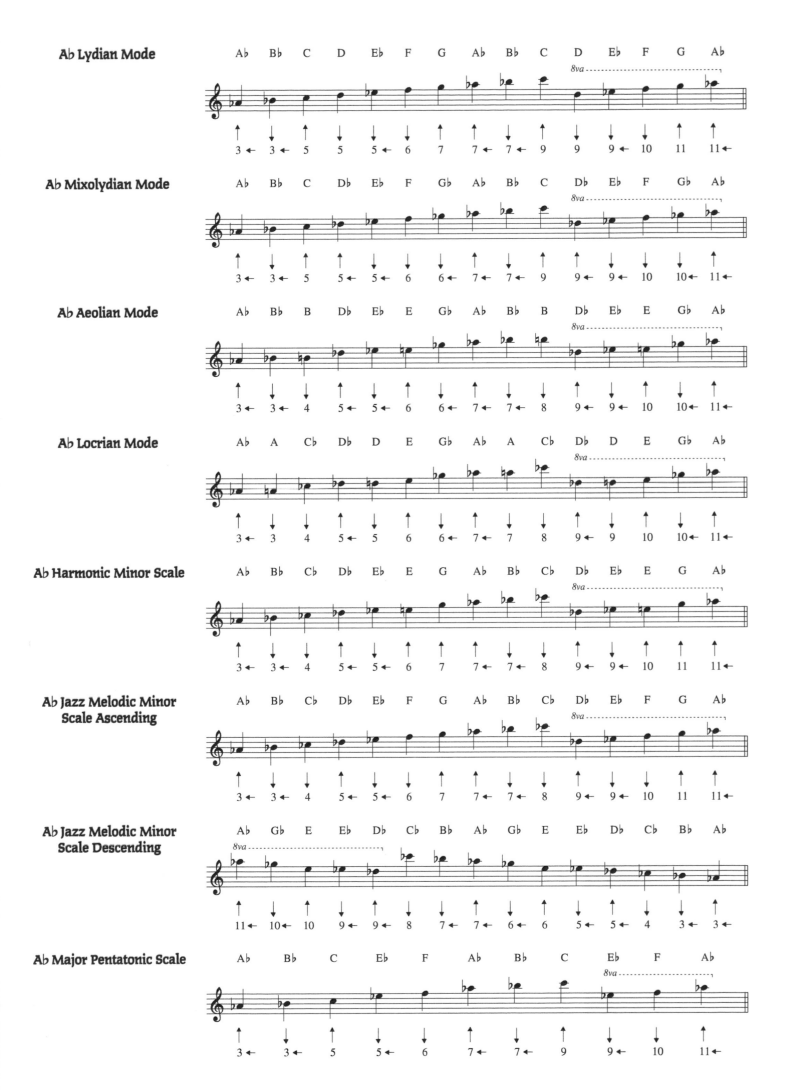

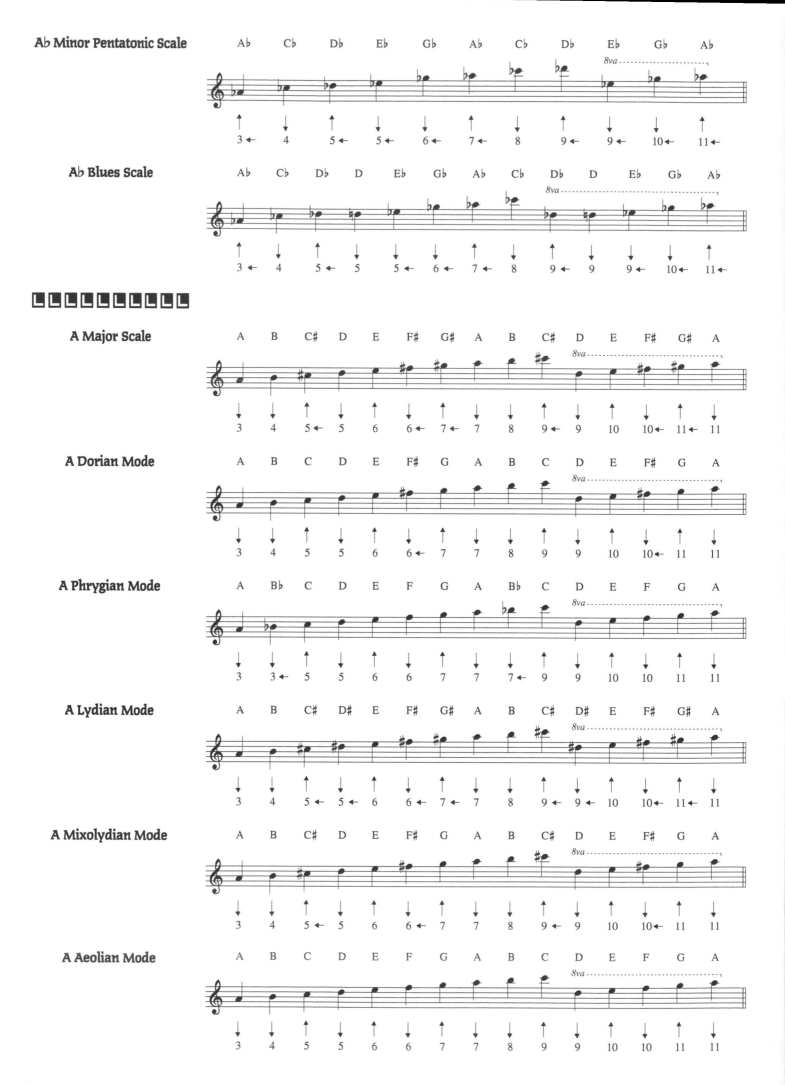

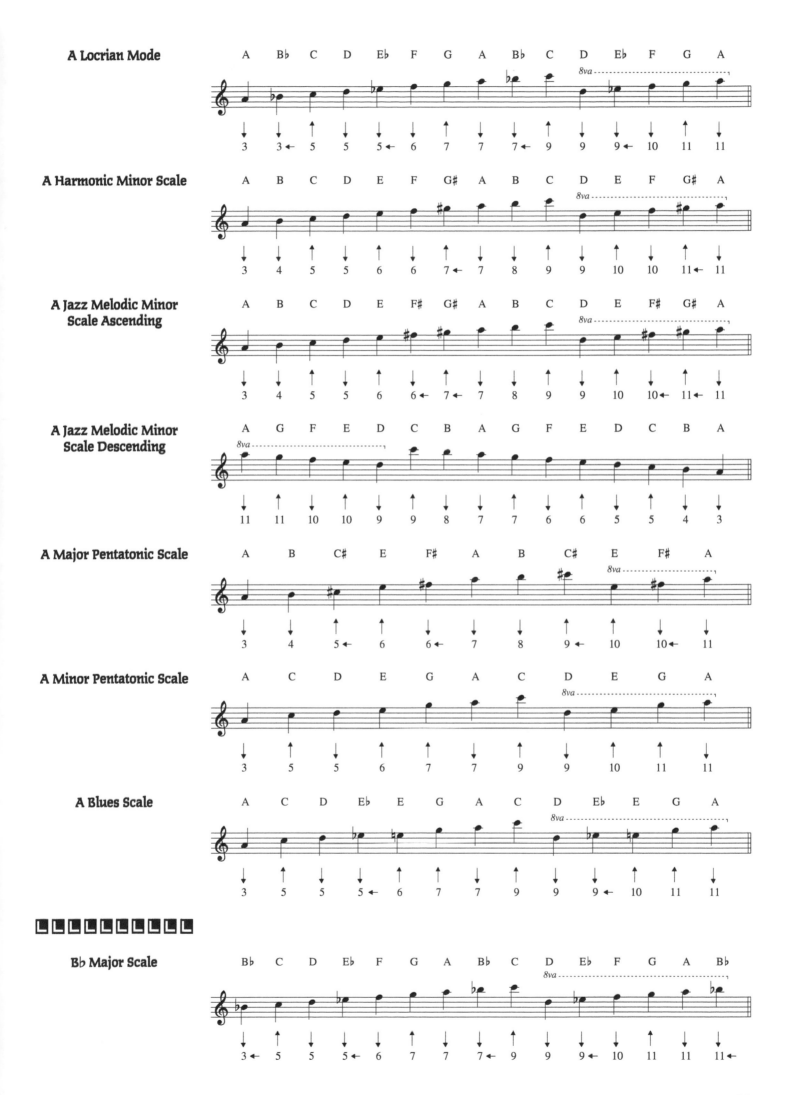

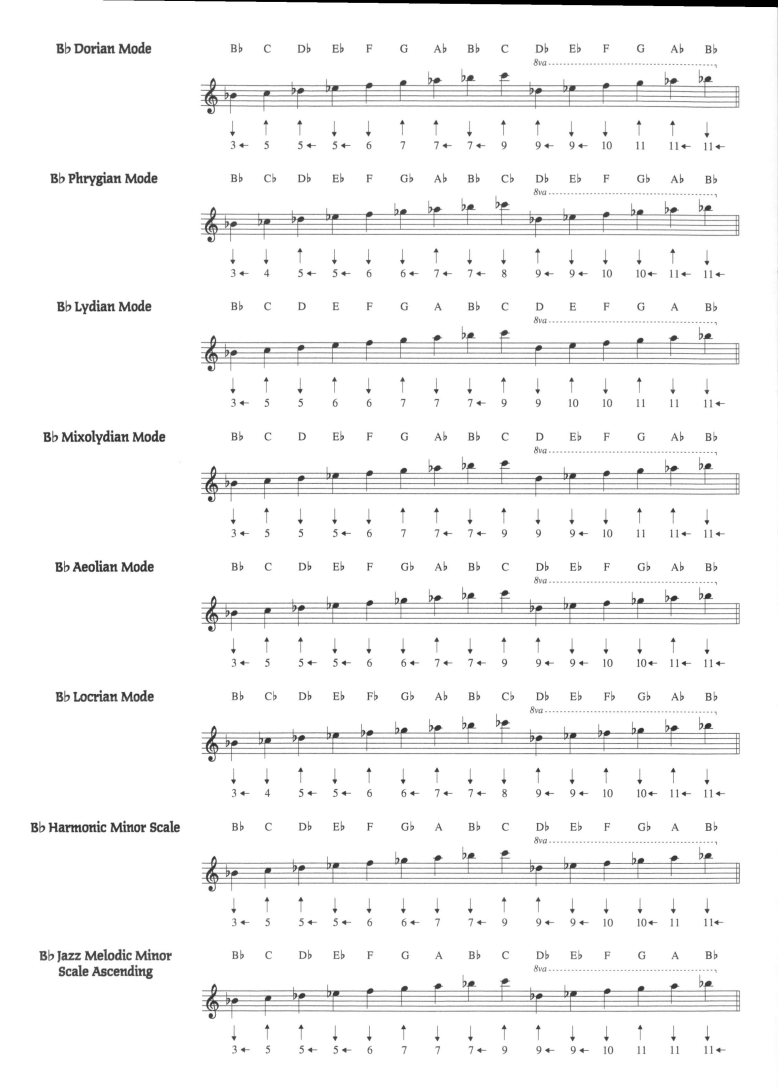

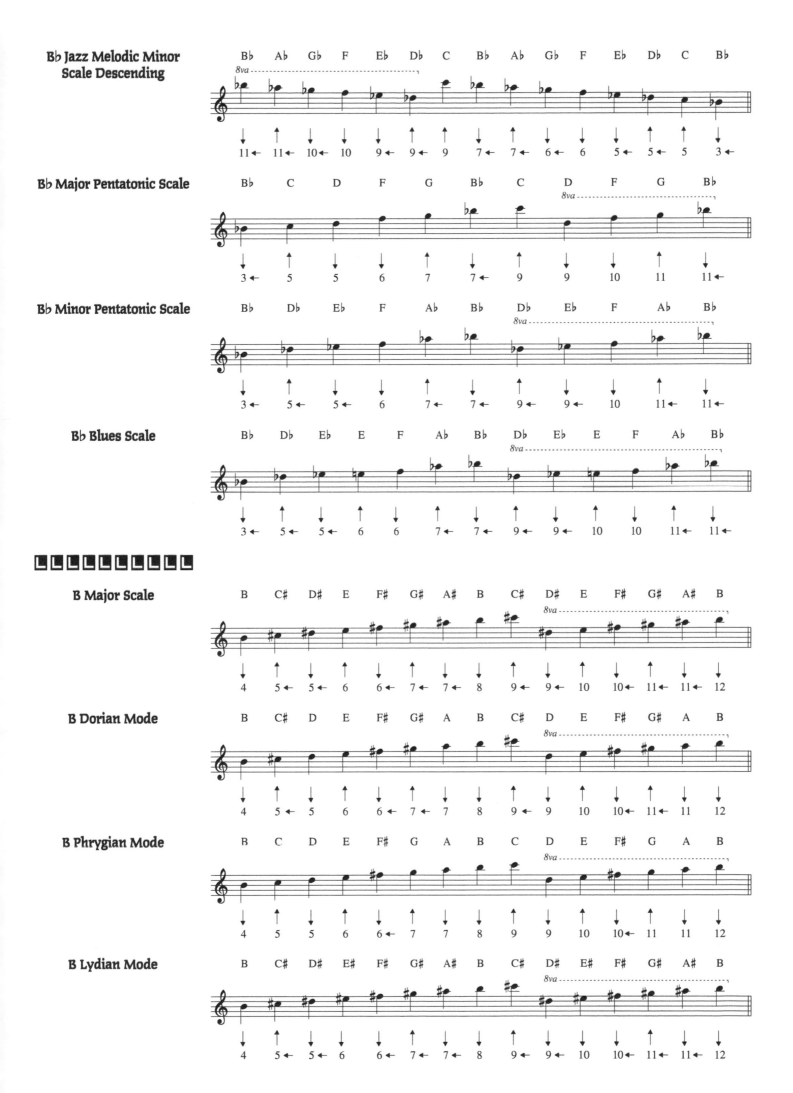

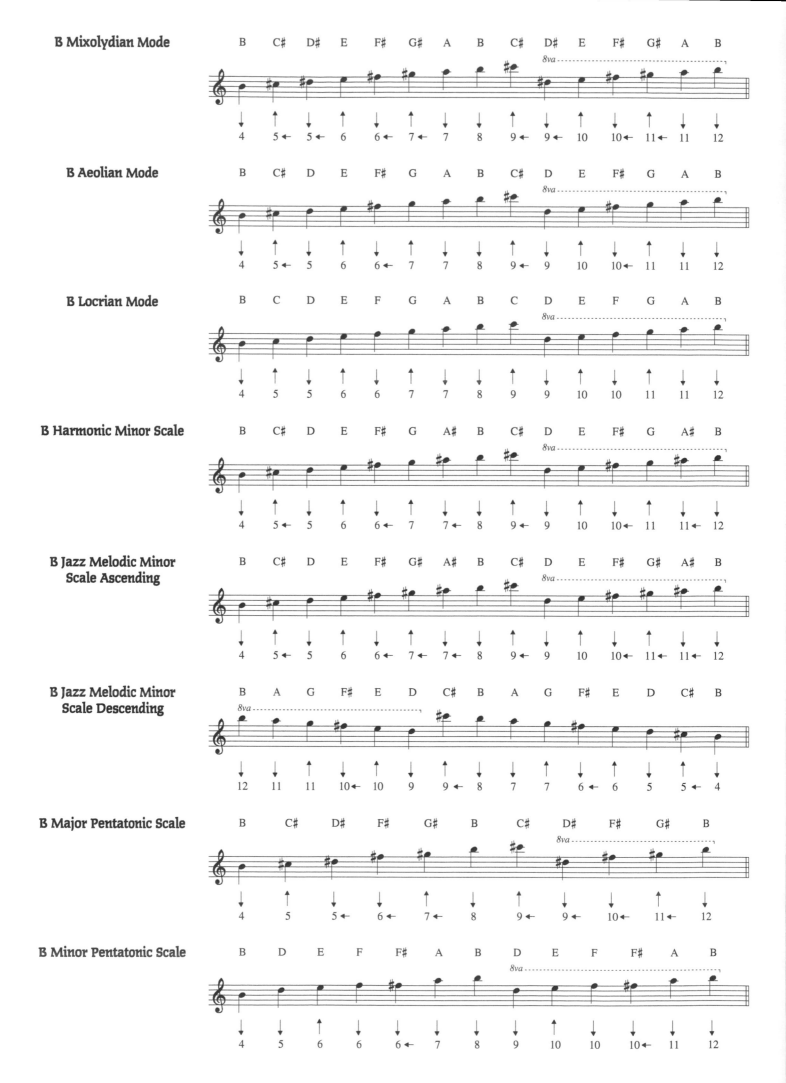

About the Author

Just for a moment, close your eyes and picture yourself listening to a sweet melodic sound. Listen as the sound changes into a myriad of gutsy, soulful riffs, slowly easing out into a journey of new imaginative heights. You now have a clear impression of a seasoned, multi-talented musician.

His name is Bobby Joe Holman. Those who are fortunate enough to hear him play his harmonica or who jam with him will say "…here is a regular kind of guy who makes you feel good inside and out, every time you see him perform."

While in his early teens, Bobby Joe first heard Paul Butterfield play the blues on the harmonica, and from that moment on, he knew he was destined to play. He began with a $1.25 harmonica, trying to imitate everything that he heard. It took him a few years, but he finally got to the point where he began to play in clubs and at parties.

He has built a career centered around the harmonica – his performances have spanned to albums, CDs, commercials, documentaries and movies. He has performed with various bands from Louisiana to California. He has endorsements with Fender, Hohner Harmonica and C.A.D. Technologies (an astatic harmonica microphone company). He has a publishing agreement with the worldwide sheet music giant, Hal Leonard Corporation.

Bobby Joe has shared his love for the harmonica with countless students over the years, many of whom have gone on to perform. His instructional video *Playing Nothin' but the Blues* has just been released, and is the next step for the harmonica student who wants to learn how to play "The Blues on the Electric Harp." Bobby Joe brings fun into the classroom and truly believes anyone can learn to play the harmonica.

THE HAL LEONARD HARMONICA METHOD AND SONGBOOKS

THE METHOD

THE HAL LEONARD COMPLETE HARMONICA METHOD — CHROMATIC HARMONICA

by Bobby Joe Holman

The only harmonica method to present the chromatic harmonica in 14 scales and modes in all 12 keys! This book will take beginners from the basics on through to the most advanced techniques available for the contemporary harmonica player. Each section contains appropriate songs and exercises that enable the player to quickly learn the various concepts presented. Every aspect of this versatile musical instrument is explored and explained in easy-to-understand detail with illustrations. The musical styles covered include traditional, blues, pop and rock.

00841286 Book/Online Audio............................. $12.99

THE HAL LEONARD COMPLETE HARMONICA METHOD — DIATONIC HARMONICA

by Bobby Joe Holman

The only harmonica method specific to the diatonic harmonica, covering all six positions. This book/audio pack contains over 20 songs and musical examples that take beginners from the basics on through to the most advanced techniques available for the contemporary harmonica player. Each section contains appropriate songs and exercises (which are demonstrated through the online video) that enable the player to quickly learn the various concepts presented. Every aspect of this versatile musical instrument is explored and explained in easy-to-understand detail with illustrations. The musical styles covered include traditional, blues, pop and rock.

00841285 Book/Online Audio............................. $12.99

THE SONGBOOKS

The Hal Leonard Harmonica Songbook series offers a wide variety of music especially tailored to the two-volume Hal Leonard Harmonica Method, but can be played by all harmonica players, diatonic and chromatic alike. All books include study and performance notes, and a guide to harmonica tablature. From classical themes to Christmas music, rock and roll to Broadway, there's something for everyone!

BROADWAY SONGS FOR HARMONICA   INCLUDES TAB

arranged by Bobby Joe Holman

19 show-stopping Broadway tunes for the harmonica. Songs include: Ain't Misbehavin' • Bali Ha'i • Camelot • Climb Ev'ry Mountain • Do-Re-Mi • Edelweiss • Give My Regards to Broadway • Hello, Dolly! • I've Grown Accustomed to Her Face • The Impossible Dream (The Quest) • Memory • Oklahoma • People • and more.
00820009...$9.95

CLASSICAL FAVORITES FOR HARMONICA   INCLUDES TAB

arranged by Bobby Joe Holman

18 famous classical melodies and themes, arranged for diatonic and chromatic players. Includes: By the Beautiful Blue Danube • Clair De Lune • The Flight of the Bumble Bee • Gypsy Rondo • Moonlight Sonata • Surprise Symphony • The Swan (Le Cygne) • Waltz of the Flowers • and more, plus a guide to harmonica tablature.
00820006..$10.99

MOVIE FAVORITES FOR HARMONICA   INCLUDES TAB

arranged by Bobby Joe Holman

19 songs from the silver screen, arranged for diatonic and chromatic harmonica. Includes: Alfie • Bless the Beasts and Children • Chim Chim Cher-ee • The Entertainer • Georgy Girl • Midnight Cowboy • Moon River • Picnic • Speak Softly, Love • Stormy Weather • Tenderly • Unchained Melody • What a Wonderful World • and more, plus a guide to harmonica tablature.
00820014 ....$9.95

HAL•LEONARD®

Visit Hal Leonard Online at
www.halleonard.com